The
Necessary
Nine

**Other Abingdon Press Books by
Bob Farr and Kay Kotan**

*Ten Prescriptions for a Healthy Church
Get Their Name
Renovate or Die*

The Necessary Nine

Things Effective Pastors Do Differently

Bob Farr
Kay Kotan

Foreword by Tex Sample

Abingdon Press

Nashville

Library of Congress Cataloging-in-Publication Data has been requested.

ISBN: 978-1-5018-0496-0

16 17 18 19 20 21 22 23 24 25—10 9 8 7 6 5 4 3 2 1
MANUFACTURED IN THE UNITED STATES OF AMERICA

Contents

Nine Things Effective Pastors Do Differently

Two Traits of Effective Congregations

Foreword

People who know Bob Farr and me will be surprised that I'm writing a foreword for this book. Bob is seen as a right-winger and I as a left-winger. He is seen as an evangelical and I as one preoccupied with the social character of the gospel. He is seen as a fundamentalist, which he is not, and I am seen as one who dismisses scripture, which I do not.

People don't know that he and I met early in his ministry. He showed up at one of my courses having done all of his work but three credit hours at another seminary. The bishop of the Missouri Annual Conference of The United Methodist Church had instructed him to come home for an appointment and to finish those three credit hours at Saint Paul School of Theology. He didn't want to do that, but he did. In my class his facial expressions conveyed his distaste in being there, and I figured it had to do with me. He didn't like me, and I didn't like him. We just made the best of a bad situation.

Recently, he and I made a big mistake. We visited and talked with each other for four hours while I consulted with him about Trinity United Methodist Church in Kansas City, Missouri, where I was serving as an interim pastor. I found that he didn't fit any of my stereotypes and that he actually knew a great deal about church starts and church renewal. Not only that, but—

speaking of miracles—I liked him. I discovered that he was not to the right of Attila the Hun but was rather a moderate who seemed to give himself to a passionate attempt at fulfilling the purpose of The United Methodist Church "to make disciples of Jesus Christ for the transformation of the world." Strangely, I didn't disagree with him about a single suggestion he made. In fact, so far as I can tell, neither of us had a single disagreement. I was so shocked, I bought his lunch!

Then I made a second mistake. I read all of his books and discovered in them an approach to church and ministry that I found remarkable—particularly the way in which he comes up with very concrete, practical steps and practices for the church to build relationships with and reach people beyond ecclesiastical walls. I see many books where authors turn to abstractions when it comes to recommendations of what to do. Farr doesn't shrink from the challenge of naming explicit avenues for action—a quality I love. In fact, I find his work so useful that I now use his material in my lectures. I even give him credit.

The partnership between Bob Farr and Kay Kotan has been creative, and they each complement the other in their work. Kotan's skill as a coach, consultant, trainer, speaker, and writer enriches the work that the two of them do together. They are both deeply experienced in this significant work.

So, if you're looking for practical, concrete suggestions for the mission and ministry of your church, this is a good place to start. But don't stop here; look at the body of work these two authors and practitioners have done together. And, when you use their stuff (as you will), give them credit.

Tex Sample
Robert B. and Kathleen Rogers Professor Emeritus of Church and Society
Saint Paul School of Theology

Acknowledgments

This book is dedicated to

Bob's mentors:
    Rev. Ray Hennigh
    Rev. Dr. Harold Dodds
    Rev. Marie Hyatt
    Rev. Kathleen Baskin-Ball

The dedicated laypeople of the congregations Bob has served, including the following:
    W. W. "Nick" and Joanne Kennedy
    Dave and Connie Senften
    John and Dee Robinson
    Robert and Helen Dean Smith
    Bob's home church, Creighton United Methodist Church
    And his youth sponsors, Dick and Margie Briggs

Kay's mentors:
    Rev. James Simpson
    Cathy Wampler
    Jille Bartolome

The hundreds of congregations and pastors Bob and Kay have consulted and coached, who have made identifying these traits possible

Acknowledgments

Introduction

[Jesus] asked them, "And what about you?
Who do you say that I am?"
Peter answered, "You are the Christ." (Mark 8:29)

Are you born a leader?

For my entire life, people have said leaders are born. It's an inherent gift. We look over our lives and history and aspire to be like other great leaders. For me (Bob), that leader is Harry Truman, who lived about twenty blocks from my grandmother. I got to meet Harry Truman at the Truman Library, so I admired him as a young person. I was intrigued to study him and understand him. What I discovered is that when he was a young man, one might have been underwhelmed in his presence. He was from a small town and a poor family. Prior to his serving in the military, you wouldn't have seen leadership qualities in him. He had just as many failures as he had accomplishments. In his military service, he began to find his voice and exhibit what we might refer to as leadership qualities. A study of Harry Truman invites the question, "How does one become a leader?" Is there such a thing as a born leader? Can a person learn to be a leader?

Another inspirational leader I look up to is Jimmy Carter. He grew up on a peanut farm in Georgia, born to an average-income family. He eventually attended the Naval Academy, following in his family's military footsteps. He developed leadership skills in school with the help of some intentional grooming from instructors and others. Was Carter a born leader, or did he acquire the skills through his military and educational training?

In contrast to Truman and Carter, we might consider John F. Kennedy. He had a predisposition for leadership. He had a well-known family name with clout. He had ample opportunity and received an excellent education. Kennedy's childhood and young adulthood were filled with experiences that few other people ever have. His family's wealth was certainly a factor in his development. He must have also been shaped by his family's expectation that he would follow in the Kennedy footsteps and become a leader. Was Kennedy a "born leader," or did his family and experiences train him to be one? Or both?

When we examine key figures in the Bible, we don't seem to find many born leaders. Some were groomed to lead. Some seemed to fall into challenging situations and learned to lead by the seat of their pants. Still others were born into leadership and family pedigree and somehow messed it up! Some, in fact, became leaders despite serious faults. Jesus is the perfect example of a born leader, of course. But what about Moses, Abraham, Paul, and Isaac? Parents look into the eyes of their newborn children and wonder, *Could this child be a leader? Could this little person impact the world?*

So we circle back around to the same question. How does one become a leader? Are you born a leader, or is it an acquired skill set? Does your upbringing make the difference? Is it genetic? Is leadership determined by environment? Education? Economic opportunity?

In Dr. Henry Cloud's book *Nine Things a Leader Must Do*, he writes about three things he has discovered about leaders:

> The answer to "Who is this person?" was not a person at all. It was a way of behaving. . . .
>
> People who found what they were looking for in life seemed to do a certain set of things in common. . . .
>
> If you were not born with these patterns for leadership in place, you can learn them.[1]

Are leaders born or made? The answer seems to us to be YES! The Healthy Church Initiative process (a church and leadership transformation process—see www.HealthyChurchInitiative.com for more information) was birthed from the Missouri Conference of The United Methodist Church when Gateway Regional District Superintendent Phil Neimeyer asked these questions in 2006 of a gathered group of six pastors in St. Louis, Missouri, who were effectively leading their churches: "What do you and other successful pastors do differently that causes your churches to grow? Is this something that you can teach to other pastors?"

---

1. Henry Cloud, *Nine Things a Leader Must Do* (Nashville: Integrity House, 2006), 9–10.

After teaching the first group of pastors (in what we now refer to as a continuous learning community), it became obvious that pastors are good learners of new information. But real results at the church resulted from changed behavior, not just new information. I will never forget a first reading *Direct Hit* by Paul Borden. In his book, he refers to "leadership behavior: is a practice, not a gift."[2] In my experience working with countless pastors and laity, I have come to my own conclusions about leadership: In most mainline denominations, approximately 10 percent of pastors are what one might call "natural-born leaders." On the other end of the spectrum, approximately 20 percent have few if any natural leadership skills, and they lack the characteristics necessary to develop strong leadership practices. These pastors will probably never become great leaders. The remaining approximately 70 percent of pastors do have at least some natural abilities. They have what it takes to acquire new leadership skills but will have to change their patterns of behavior in order to be truly effective in ministry.

This book offers nine traits that I have identified as the key things pastors must do differently in order to be effective leaders in their congregations and two traits of effective congregations. I've spent a lot of time exploring the differences between effective pastors and ineffective ones and worked with many pastors who are striving to become the best leaders they can be. I agree with Cloud that it's less about the "who" and more about the "what." It's less about natural abilities and more about practices, patterns, habits, attitudes, and tactics. John Wesley would refer

---

2. Paul Borden, *Direct Hit: Aiming Real Leaders at the Mission Field* (Nashville: Abingdon Press, 2006), 30.

to these practices as a "way of life."[3] Methodism was a set of patterns and practices that Wesley felt produced the Christian way of life. Effectiveness is a way of life. I appreciate the value of knowledge and learning, as did Wesley. However, I am a practitioner more than a theologian or an academic. In my experience, it's the practice of a certain set of behaviors that changes everything for pastors and their congregations.

This book outlines nine practices that effective pastors and leaders do differently and the two things effective congregations do differently. They are the patterns of behavior that I have practiced myself and have seen other effective pastors practice. I have also seen what happens when pastors do not practice these behaviors, leading to immense struggles in ministry. I chose these nine because they are often overlooked, ignored, or not commonly practiced. My prayer is that pastors and other leaders will begin to change and grow as a result of this book so that their churches will thrive. In our previous book *Renovate or Die* (2011), we wrote about having to change the church before you can change the world. It has become apparent to me in the last eight years of my ministry as the Director of Congregational Excellence, where I have consulted and coached with hundreds of churches, that you have to change the pastors and leaders before you can change the church.

Bob Farr

---

3. John Wesley, "The Way To The Kingdom," Wesley Center Online, http://wesley .nnu.edu/john-wesley/the-sermons-of-john-wesley-1872-edition/sermon-7-the-way-to -the-kingdom/.

The last two chapters of this book identify two traits of effective congregations. These traits become multiplying factors—power boosters, of sorts—when they are coupled with the nine practices of effective pastors. When an effective pastor leads an effective congregation, the possibilities are limitless. On the other hand, if a pastor arrives at a church where these two traits are not present, it's incredibly difficult for the church and pastor to be effective, even if the pastor is practicing the nine traits.

Pastors are more effective when they're practicing the nine traits. Congregations are more effective when they're practicing the two traits. When an effective pastor and an effective congregation are in the same place, watch out! When this happens, there is a bountiful harvest of fruit and effectiveness, and more people come to know Jesus Christ through the life of the congregation. This sort of church is a great place to be; it deepens people's lives and changes the community and the world. And folks, that's what it's all about, isn't it?

Kay Kotan

9

Nine Things Effective Pastors Do Differently

Chapter One

Show Up and Move In

The Word became flesh and made his home among us. We have seen his glory, glory like that of a father's only Son, full of grace and truth. (John 1:14)

Recently, I went back and interviewed laity from three of the five congregations I have served in my thirty-seven-year history in ministry. I asked what I did differently than other pastors that caused them and the congregations to go in new directions and try new ministries. I thought I already knew the answer to my own questions. As it turned out, I did know most of the answers. But there were surprises along the way. The best one-liner response that surprised me came from one particular congregant, W. W. "Nick" Kennedy. He said, "You showed up." I asked, "Didn't every pastor show up?" He responded, "Yes, but you also moved in . . . to our lives." I asked, "What do you mean?" Nick and Joanne Kennedy both cited multiple stories of how I became involved in the lives of their families, the lives of the congregation, and the lives of the community. In all the interviews, it became obvious that the first trait of an effective pastor is the ability to integrate himself or herself into the very fabric of the congregation and community he or she has moved into. This is the absolute first trait you must live into. If you don't, the congregation won't allow you to engage in the other activities that you need to accomplish in order to be effective.

It's not how much you know but how much you care. This is essential in the beginning of any pastoral ministry. I have never met a pastor who didn't care about her or his congregation. Yet this is a deeper investment than I see most pastors willing to commit to. I move into a congregation with the attitude that this is the last church I may ever get to serve, so I better pour it all in. If you want to get buy-in from a congregation, you as pastor have to be all in. It is taking ownership and responsibility for the congregation and community. It is intertwining your life with their life. It is seeing more than just the congregation but rather the community as your mission field. Some pastors drive into a community and all they see is the church they have been assigned to serve. Others drive into the community and see all of the houses around the church and ache with a burden to do something to reach the neighborhood beyond just pastoring the church. It drives me crazy to visit communities where I previously served and see the vibrant neighborhoods but the church closed or dwindling. For when you are all in, you can't help wanting to do something beyond just playing church. There must be a deep conviction in one's soul to help people know Jesus Christ beyond just serving the local church. When a church moves out beyond its own walls, any church can become a compelling congregation.

One of the essentials of showing up and moving in is, in fact, "living the mission field." What I mean by this is networking. All my life I have heard, "Work on getting your church in order or 'well' before you go out into your mission field and invite people in." There is some truth to that. However, what I have done is to go out into the mission field and start making connections, networking, elbowing people to the church, and building new relations. In my experience, this will actually begin to get your church in order. It is more effective to start on the outside and work in rather than starting on the inside and working outward. Perhaps it is simultaneous work, inside your church and also outside in the mission field. Take one hand and help your congregation become more missional while you take the other hand to reach the mission field. Living the mission field, for me, is shopping at the local businesses. It is walking your dog in the neighborhood. It is getting acquainted at the local elementary school and volunteering there. It is hanging out at the local coffee shop. It is getting involved in organizations in your community where unchurched people are members. It is hanging out at the gym. It is asking people to introduce you to other people in the community. It is following God's tug at your heart to start conversations with people you don't know.

All of these things are easier when you actually physically live in the mission field, but a pastor could certainly live "with" the mission field even without living in the mission field itself. I do think that if at all possible, one ought to actually live in the mission field. This says something about your buy-in to the local community and it makes it much, much easier to hang out in your community when you live there rather than driving in.

While living the mission is the first step of being an effective pastor, it is closely followed by an attitude: I want to be here! As I interviewed other laity from the congregations I have served, there was a continual theme about enthusiasm. Most people just said I was enthusiastic about being at their church, which was contagious from day one. I have often said to people who ask how I grew my churches that in the first half of ministry I simply did Methodism enthusiastically. This was very different from what they had experienced in their previous pastoral leadership. What they had experienced was Methodism done lethargically. My churches grew even though we didn't have contemporary worship. We didn't have the greatest locations or buildings. We didn't have great resources. I didn't have a lot of experience in church growth. We didn't have the youngest leaders and not everybody was helpful. In fact, some dragged their feet at every turn to make sure that nothing changed. Yet enthusiasm carried the day. To this day, when faced by some negativity around decisions, ideas people don't like, actions that are unpopular, and mistakes I have personally made, I overcome these with being enthusiastic. I am reminded that the root word of *enthusiasm* is "with God." When you look up *enthusiasm* in Google, it says, "early 17th century . . . : from French *enthousiasme*, or via late Latin from Greek *enthousiasmos*, from *enthous* 'possessed by a god, inspired' (based on *theos* 'god')." Also *enthusiasm* is described as "intense and eager enjoyment, interest, or approval . . . 'her energy and **enthusiasm for** life.'" Synonyms listed include, "eagerness, keenness, ardor, fervor, passion, zeal, zest, gusto, energy, verve, vigor, vehemence, fire, spirit, avidity," and "religious fervor supposedly resulting directly from divine inspiration."[1]

Enthusiasts, where are you? Let us be reminded that we United Methodists were once called enthusiasts. Enthusiasts, where did you go? Looking at Google's antonyms for *enthusi-*

---

1. "enthusiasm," Google, https://www.google.com/search?q=enthusiasm&oq=enthusiasm&aqs=chrome..69i57j0l5.783j0j7&sourceid=chrome&es_sm=91&ie=UTF-8.

asm, you find "apathy" and "half-heartedness." I am certain that the early Methodist circuit riders' enthusiasm contributed to our early growth and impact on the culture. I have always wondered when people quit calling us enthusiasts and we became a passive denomination. People have heard me say, "You may not like what I have to say, but you are going to know I showed up!" **Are you all in?**

Enthusiasm won't cure everything. That's for sure! But it is hard to imagine an effective ministry without enthusiasm. Enthusiasm reveals itself in different ways for different people. Mine shows up in action and attitude. It is outwardly obvious. Yet I have met very effective pastors who are introverts whose enthusiasm shows up in different ways. They are no less passionate, driven, and invested in their settings, which results in effectiveness.

Where enthusiasm shows itself most is in worship experiences. This includes not only the sermon, but how you engage with the people in the lobby, at the front door, and in the worship service itself. It is how you carry yourself that makes you approachable. The service itself has energy and the pastor has energy. Too many times I attend worship and experience a lethargic atmosphere all around. It feels like people are just going through the motions. The biggest game changer for the Sunday morning experience can be the pastor. When the pastor enters with energy and enthusiasm, it is contagious to other people. This is so important because how worship goes affects everything else in the life of the congregation during the week. Without enthusiasm on Sunday morning, every other ministry begins to wane.

This is a people business. I don't know how you show up and move in if you don't have a burden for people and their knowing Jesus Christ. All my life, people have called me an evangelical. What I think most interpret that to mean is having a conservative theology. If you knew me very well, you would know that is not true. I am a centrist theologian (light on theologian and heavy on practitioner). I am an evangelical in the sense that I believe having an experience and relationship with Jesus Christ (whatever that means to you) is a key to a purposeful and meaningful life. I have a burden for helping people who do not have that relationship to find a relationship with Jesus. I have a deep belief that the role of the church is to be a bridge from where people are to a relationship with Jesus Christ. I do not believe the church is a place of destination. Rather the church is a place of connection—connecting people from where they are to where they need to go. So, you show up and move in with a heart for the people—all people inside and outside the church. This means throwing our hearts wide open to anybody and everybody in the neighborhoods that surround the church and the various neighborhoods of our lives. It is networking, networking, networking. It is enthusiasm and attitude. It is a positive spirit trusting that this is the very place God wants me to be even if I have a few doubts about it myself. It is about showing up and moving in. Are you all in—in every way? Is this a job for you or is it your way of life?

Listen Up and Lead with Your Ears

Know this, my dear brothers and sisters: everyone should be quick to listen, slow to speak, and slow to grow angry. This is because an angry person doesn't produce God's righteousness. (James 1:19-20)

I listened my way through the world. (Organizer Bob Moses)

When I interviewed the laity at three of my previous churches, one of the top traits they identified very quickly was my ability to hear their story and to listen. Not only was I listening for their story, but I was also listening for what their passions and talents revealed about what role they could play in the new future we were going to build together. I refer to this as listening with a purpose. I often advise pastors when they are going to their new church assignment/appointment to have the Pastor-Parish Relations (PPR) team (or whatever the personnel equivalent in your church is) create a series of chats (cottage conversations, coffees with the pastor, and so forth) between the new pastor and members of the congregation. Many pastors have casual conversations, which is fine, but what I am suggesting are conversations with a purpose. The purpose of these chats is multifaceted. One is to be acquainted with one another. The second is the opportunity for me to ask intentional questions. Here are some examples of those questions:

- What is your name? How long have you been here? Which service do you attend? What is the ministry you like to do?

- What is the best thing about this church?

- What is the one thing you would like to change about your church?

- What is your hope for the future of the church? Where would you like to see the church in three years?

- Who are the two or three people I need to go visit right now?

- If you were the new pastor here, what would be the first thing you would do?

I have someone take notes for me so I am not sidetracked from the conversation yet have the information captured. This is the first step to engage with the congregation and get to know them. If at all possible, I have a conversation with the PPR/personnel team prior to my arrival to arrange these pastor chats. These chats commence within a week of showing up and moving in. In fact, this is part of the "moving in."

The truth is, prior to arriving you need to listen up. This occurs by learning as much as you can about your new mission field. You can do this by researching Mission Insite (which provides demographic reports), reading the history of the area, reading the history of the church, researching the local chamber of commerce and school district websites, researching the area's major employers, discovering who their sports teams are, reading the local paper, and going to social media sites to learn all you can about the area. Part of listening up is learning about your context and your church.

Listening up requires listening to both inside voices and outside voices. The pastor chats are an example of listening to inside voices. The second step of the inside listening is to talk to every elected leader and key influencers in the church. Again this is not a casual conversation. They are intentional conversations with a purpose. Most of the questions for the leaders are around "How do things work around here?" It is much better to find out this information prior to making a misstep, especially if you are as prone to action as I am.

If you only listen to inside voices, you will have a biased view of your mission field. Most churches are not as connected to their immediate community as they believe they are. The fact is, listening up requires you to get a new read on the community and culture around the church building. Often when a church grows up in a community, they think they know that community. However, churches many times become insular and disconnected over the course of time due to changes within that very community. So it becomes important, as a new person, to get a new read on the community as quickly as possible. You, too, will quickly become isolated from the community because we all have the natural instinct to form habits and patterns that shape what we believe to be true about the community we live in.

Listening up to outside voices is also multifaceted. The first step in listening to outside voices would include intentional conversations with the nearest school principal, fire chief, police chief, mayor, city council members, social service leaders, chamber of commerce leaders, leaders of other civic clubs, and so on. Examples of things to say and ask are the following:

- Tell me about your organization.

- Who do you serve?

- What are the most pressing needs of the community?

- What do you know about the church I serve?

- How could the church be helpful?

The second step in listening up to outside voices is to walk the business district introducing yourself and asking questions. Examples of things to say and ask are the following:

- Tell me about your business.

- Who is your customer base?

- Where are your customers mostly from?

- What are the traffic patterns around here?

- What are the greatest opportunities in this community?

• What do you know about the church I serve?

• How could the church be helpful?

   The third step in listening up to outside voices is to prayer-walk the neighborhoods. This is the only step where I ask the congregation to participate with me. I don't press people to go. I invite people. I don't get too worried about how many come because this is very early in the relationship with the congregation. Also this is probably asking them to do something they have not previously experienced and are unsure about. You probably don't have enough trust built up yet to convince a whole lot of people to participate. Here are some examples of some activities during a prayer walk:

• Hand out water bottles to your neighbors in the yard and introduce yourself.

• If you get into a conversation with someone, ask them some of the following questions.

   o   What is your name?

   o   How long have you lived here?

   o   What are your interests?

   o   What do you know about the church I serve?

   o   Do you have a church home?

   o   What could our church do to be helpful?

   o   Can I pray with you? Anything specific?

• Stop in front of houses and pray.

• Pray with the team (if you have one) before you go out.
  Debrief and pray with the team on your return.

The reason for these questions is to determine the reputation of the church, turnover rate in the neighborhood, interests of the community, and the church attendance factor. This is a way to confirm the Mission Insite demographic information at the street level. I refer to this as gathering the walk-around information. This is a couple of hours on a late Saturday morning or early afternoon or on a late Sunday afternoon (times may vary according to culture).

The art of listening up is first about hearing someone else's story. It is about a genuine interest in other people. It is an investment in other people. It is a passion for the people you are called to serve. If you want to be effective in a congregation, you can only do that to the degree that you genuinely invest in the people. If you want to build trust, you must demonstrate a deep, authentic pastoral care. Yet, you cannot get so wrapped up in pastoral care that you fail to accomplish the ministry tasks you need to do to have an effective ministry. If you invest early in pastoral care and building trust, the congregation will more likely let you set up a pastoral care system where the congregation cares for one another as you move to reaching new people and other ministries. Be careful here, because most congregations will let you care for them until the cows come home. They will think you are a great pastor, but your congregation will decline in attendance. This will most likely not result in an effective ministry if gaining new people for Jesus Christ is one of your goals.

In the art of listening up and leading with your ears, you are attempting to build trust. Building trust is imperative. It allows you to deposit trust coins in your pastoral bank account. Trust is the currency of a local church. When there is no trust between the pastor and the congregation, it is very hard to move forward. When there is no trust between the leadership and the congregation, it often leads to tension, conflict, rumors, and a whole host of dysfunctional behaviors within the congregation. When there is little or no trust between the pastor and leadership, there is little chance to get any amount of change accomplished. It is very rare for a congregation to produce new fruit without having to live through some significant changes in how they approach ministry. So without trust, it is hard to enact changes, which in turn limits our effectiveness.

A deeper level of listening up is not just task-driven (that is, having a nice, passive conversation). It is about having a conversation with a mission in mind. It is an intentional conversation. Where can we collaborate to bring about more effectiveness and future alignment with the mission? Even with the outsiders, I circle back multiple times over the course of the year. I do this with the mission in mind. It is a genuine, authentic investment in people and in listening, but it is with a mission in mind and not just for fun. Jesus had few conversations without a mission in mind. There was a purpose in his conversations—a way of life. His conversations and his listening always led somewhere.

Both the inside and outside listening up leads to engaging people in their own ministry. By investing in people and listening to them, I am more easily able to connect people with other people and with ministry that fits their interests, skills, and affinity. The ability to engage people and teams in ministry is greatly

15

dependent on you knowing your people. Without listening up, you do not have a deep enough connection with your people to help find their ministry role. It continues to amaze me how pastors struggle to assemble teams within the congregation. This would seem to be a symptom that a pastor has not fully engaged and invested in their people by listening up. In larger churches, it is apparent that listening up is not happening when leaders and staff are working tirelessly doing ministry themselves rather than identifying and equipping other leaders who recruit volunteers to help in ministry.

There seems to be a lone-wolf mentality in our clergy and lay leadership in the midst of a tribe (denomination) that is supposedly a connectional system. The art of listening up and leading with your ears also lends itself to looking for answers from any and all directions from all people. There is no way one person has all the answers to all the questions. By listening up, you are building up an arsenal of people and connections with varied skills, experiences, and gifts who can be helpful in your ministry. Anybody who knows me knows that I have an opinion on just about everything. They might, in fact, mistake my having an opinion about everything with my having an answer to everything. However, if you worked with me very long you would confirm I do indeed have an opinion about everything, but I seek answers from any and all directions. I constantly ask questions and inquire about best practices. People are flabbergasted by the number of phone calls I make and receive each day, the number of people I confer with, and the number of people I know in general. This has, of course, happened over time through my willingness to listen up and to engage people where they are. This has proven to be very beneficial in every level of ministry I have been involved in from the congregational work to my judicatory work. I am not afraid to have the very best people around me at all times. I am not afraid of having people far more qualified than me surrounding me. I prefer to hire up. The brighter the people I have around me, the smarter I look. Though I have an opinion, I am confident and clear that I do not have all the answers. In fact, the best answers come when I have listened up and led with my ears.

Listening up starts with being approachable. Approachability is partly about being accessible. Ministry is often described as a life of interruptions. If you don't build in any margins in your life for interruptions, you may appear to be unapproachable. You have to be careful with this or you will find yourself spending all your time on the "urgent" rather than the "important" things that would hinder effective ministry. This is an open-door policy for the most part. Although I have had to learn how to shut the door and create nonapproachable times to get the "important" (yet not urgent) things completed, most people coming into any place I serve, whether a church or the conference office I serve in now, have a sense that if I'm not already occupied, they in fact can approach me with anything. Without creating a culture of approachability with yourself and throughout your whole organization, you will not be afforded the opportunity to listen up and lead with your ears. An organization with a culture of approachability has the beginnings of a culture of transparency and the opportunity to become authentic.

The art of listening up and leading with your ears requires intentionality and some organization. It begins by getting to know your context, listening to inside and outside voices, connecting, and hearing people's stories. We are in a people business.

It includes an understanding that engaging and connecting with a variety of people will help the church find the mission as well as help you accomplish the mission. Trust is a product of listening up. Trust is the currency of a church at all levels. None of us has all of the answers. Yet most answers lie somewhere within the people you are connected with and those you have yet to connect with. Connections begin with approachability and availability. Have you created enough margin in your life to be approachable and available to listen up and lead with your ears on purpose?

Chapter Three

Adopt a Bias for Action

9

What I mean is this: the one who sows a small number of seeds will also reap a small crop, and the one who sows a generous amount of seeds will also reap a generous crop.
(2 Corinthians 9:6)

Walk the talk!

One of the things you need to understand when you arrive at a church as a new pastor is that most of the time the congregation has been suffering from years of stagnation and/or decline (if you are in a mainline church). There is a deep erosion of confidence in most congregations. The fact is, most congregations are looking in their rearview mirror seeing their best days behind them.

As the new pastor, you are faced with creating momentum in a culture that has not seen a "winning season" in years. I am a Kansas City Royals fan. After twenty-nine seasons of nonsuccess, there was not one player on the 2014 team who had been in the club house in 1985, when the team had last had a winning

19

tradition. Therefore, it was very difficult to believe as a fan (and I suspect as a player) that this franchise could once again be in the pennant race. It seemed like every spring the Royals franchise would run a marketing campaign that would insinuate that this was "our year." Yet, year after year, it was not. So it was very hard to believe in 2014 that this really was "our year." As the 2014 season progressed, there were more and more hopeful signs that maybe this could indeed be "our year." Throughout the season, the team along with the fans picked up momentum. As the fall turned, so did the fortunes of the Kansas City Royals. Even with the wins, some of the "fair-weather fans" were still not on the bandwagon. It had been a long time since there had been a real winning season. Momentum comes with some wins and can change the course of any organization. For example, the momentum from 2014 created a winning season for the Royals' in 2015. One win builds on another until you get a winning tradition. But it's hard to believe in something when it's been a long time since the church has had a real winning season. How many times has a new program or initiative come along in the church promising a real winning season, only for the congregation to once again be disappointed in the results? I live in St. Louis. It is very easy to believe that the Cardinals could win. They have a winning tradition for decades. It is hard to believe they could not win.

Pastors and churches face the same thing. It is hard to believe that an organization could once again be competent and compelling after years of malaise and apathy—"nonwinning seasons and traditions." In these churches, when the new pastor brings up new ideas with the hopes of a winning season, he or she is likely to hear, "We've already tried that" or "That never works around here" or "We've never done it that way." This is another way of saying we've tried stuff and it never worked or it is hard to believe we could have a "winning season." Yet, action needs to be taken if the organization is going to find a new future.

What changes momentum in a game? You have to change something! You have to take a different action. If you keep taking the same actions over and over again expecting a different outcome, you are living into the definition of insanity!

What begins to change the culture of decline is getting a few small wins. In order to get a few wins, we must create some urgency. Creating urgency starts with brutal honesty about the current reality of the church. The current reality is discovered through the homework the pastor does before showing up at the church and moving in, and through living with the church and in the mission field. Current reality without future hope simply depresses people. So you must be ready with one or two steps that would produce some small wins that point to a new future. Some of the most obvious first steps become apparent in the listening sessions from chapter 2. In some churches, urgency meets you at the front door. Yet in other churches, the malaise and decline have been so slow and drawn out, you have to create the urgency. The congregation has become very comfortable in their decline. It is their "normal" and they have gotten used to their situation. The congregation knows in their bones that they are less than they used to be, but nobody talks about it and certainly nobody wants to take dramatic action to change the status quo.

What gives most pastors the go-ahead to take action is the threefold approach mentioned in chapters 1 and 2 of showing up, moving in, and leading with your ears. Without these three previous steps, a congregation will simply not let you take the kind of actions you need to take to create a new future. On the other hand, if all you do is show up, move in, and lead with your ears without a bias for action, you will have a very loving time, but the congregation will continue to decline.

It is the bias for action that begins to change the course of the congregation. Try something! So the question becomes, what action steps do I take? What do I try? Most of the action steps I took were obvious things that needed to be fixed (such as a new carpet, air conditioning, a sound system, and signage). Notice all of these examples are technical changes—not adaptive. You don't start with adaptive change. You need small wins and these can most easily and quickly come from technical change. The second wave of changes most likely comes within the ministry and programs area, resulting from the listening sessions. This could be adding a ministry such as one to youth or children.

Most of the early actions you, as pastor, must take yourself. This is nothing short of just plain hard work. This is not a forty-hour-a-week job. This is not a job at all. In fact, if you view this as a job, you are in the wrong "job." Pastoring is a lifestyle. You don't turn it off and on. I have never seen transformation occur in a congregation with a pastor who works forty hours a week or less. I am sorry, but it just doesn't work that way! I am not saying not to take your day off. I am not saying not to set boundaries. (See chapter 5.) I am saying this takes an incredible work ethic if one is to be effective in ministry. I am probably not the smartest pastor a church has ever had, but I may be the hardest-working pastor a church ever had. In my experience, people respect other people who work hard at their profession. Most successful business people, farmers, teachers, and so on that I know have worked incredibly hard and have the same expectation of someone they are being asked to follow and invest in. To gain the respect of your congregation and community, you must have a solid work ethic. It pains me to say that in my eight years of supervisory work in the United Methodist Church, I am underwhelmed by the present work ethic in some of our clergy. They are very good people. They are moral people. They are called by God. Many of them are likely more spiritual and studious than I am. I am concerned, however, that some of our clergy may lack a strong work ethic and bias for action. This makes our congregations weak and our effectiveness a languishing dream.

To have a bias for action, you have to be willing to take some risks. You have to be willing to try something and fail. You have to be willing and able to correct your course quickly. To be a person with a bias for action, you must be open to fierce feedback and course corrections or you come across as a bull in a china closet. This is where investing in your leaders is very important. No action is taken alone. Action is most often taken in collaboration with your leadership. This is what makes you approachable. I am not suggesting a lone-wolf approach. I am suggesting an approach that involves a deep work ethic with a bias for action that seeks lots of opinions, feedback, and even some occasional loud conversations in order to gain followers. I often say you had better look behind yourself to make sure you have followers. Without followers, your actions will not be effective and you will alienate a variety of people. At the same time, you cannot be held hostage by some people not liking the actions that need to be taken. If you have a need for everyone in your congregation to like you, then this is probably not the profession for you. True leaders have a tremendous bias for action and typically an opinion about everything. But, true leaders are absolutely convinced that they do not have all the answers. They are convinced they have some of the answers. If you are not convicted about some things, then this profession is probably not for you.

Being effective in ministry is not a sprint. It is a marathon. It takes persistence. Not only does it takes persistence, it takes tenacity and a good dose of common sense. You can work really hard and not be effective. Working hard needs to be coupled with working smart on the right things. Working smart means knowing what to pay attention to and what not to pay attention to. Transformation in local congregations does not occur in three to six months. In fact, you may not begin to see fruit in your ministry until year three. But if you are not being effective by year three, you need to reevaluate to see if you are doing the right things. Most leaders begin to see effectiveness within eighteen months into their pastorate. On the other hand, if effectiveness is not occurring by year three, I rarely see it occur by year five. For the ministry fruit to multiply and have the most impact, it requires a long-term investment. The most highly effective pastorates range from seven to twenty years. Just length of time served does not necessarily mean you are effective in your ministry. Yet many of the most effective pastors do indeed bear fruit in their ministry in long tenures in the same setting.

Pastors are crafters of culture. How do you craft a culture? Crafting a culture begins with knowing your mission, understanding your vision, being able to articulate your values, strategizing your goals, and taking appropriate action. Without action, nothing happens—nothing changes. Churches have years of predictable patterns of action. If we want to see new effectiveness, a new pattern of purposeful action will need to occur. The first action step to create a culture of effectiveness must be made by the pastor, closely followed by lay leadership. In order to create a new future, you must first create a sense of urgency. Urgency comes from understanding and communicating clearly your current reality. To begin to change the current reality, take steps in order to get some small technical wins at first. Wins begin to shift the momentum of the congregation and help build confidence that indeed a new future and a winning season is possible. This will take hard work, persistence, and being open to fierce feedback as you risk failure with the chance of a new win. Effectiveness requires a bias for action. No amount of study will replace the need for action. Just knowing or reading about something does not mean that we have done it. The book of James reminds us that faith without deeds is dead:

> My brothers and sisters, what good is it if people say they have faith but do nothing to show it? Claiming to have faith can't save anyone, can it? Imagine a brother or sister who is naked and never has enough food to eat. What if one of you said, "Go in peace! Stay warm! Have a nice meal!"? What good is it if you don't actually give them what their body needs? In the same way, faith is dead when it doesn't result in faithful activity.
>
> Someone might claim, "You have faith and I have action." But how can I see your faith apart from your actions? Instead, I'll show you my faith by putting it into practice in faithful action. It's good that you believe that God is one. Ha! Even the demons believe this, and they tremble with fear. Are you so slow? Do you need to be shown that faith without actions has no value at all? (James 2:14-20)

Chapter Four

Get Spiritual

This is why I kneel before the Father. Every ethnic group in heaven or on earth is recognized by him. I ask that he will strengthen you in your inner selves from the riches of his glory through the Spirit. I ask that Christ will live in your hearts through faith. As a result of having strong roots in love, I ask that you'll have the power to grasp love's width and length, height and depth, together with all believers. I ask that you'll know the love of Christ that is beyond knowledge so that you will be filled entirely with the fullness of God.
Glory to God, who is able to do far beyond all that we could ask or imagine by his power at work within us; glory to him in the church and in Christ Jesus for all generations, forever and always. Amen. (Ephesians 3:14-21)

Every time I feel the spirit . . . I will pray. (African-American spiritual)

Reverend Kendall Waller of the Missouri Annual Conference of the United Methodist Church often states, "You can't give away what you don't have." How true this is for so many things, but how crucially true this is for a pastor leading a congregation. How easy it is to live a church

27

life and yet be spiritually detached. To paraphrase John Wesley, how easy it is to have the outer form of religion without the inner substance. We have all heard pastors say the only time they are studying the word is when they are working on a sermon. Midway through the pastoral leadership development learning process in the Missouri Annual Conference, I visited each learning group to gain feedback on topics, process, and future possibilities. I was surprised with two pieces of feedback. First, most of the 120 pastors in the groups confessed that it was very difficult to hold one another accountable. Second, most pastors found it difficult to stay spiritually grounded in the midst of church work. Many pastors were carrying quite a bit of guilt around over the feeling that it was hard to be spiritual as a pastor while operating a church when supposedly that is one of our main tenets. Many of my peers were thinking they were the only ones who could possibly be in this spot—which, of course, they were not. There is not a pastor among us who has been in the ministry for very long who has not had the dark night of the soul, each of us wondering where our own spirituality went and asking, "How could this have happened when I am a pastor?" Yet, including me, most of us as pastors hesitate to verbalize this feeling because we wonder what our peers and our congregation would think. So we don't talk about it much. Yet in the thirty-seven years I have been in full-time ministry, there has not been a single Annual Conference session when I didn't look across the sea of faces and wonder what happened to us. How did we become so hollowed out inside? How is it that by the time some of our clergy retire, they retire bitter if not angry? What's the deal?

In chapter 6 of *The Balancing Act*, Bishop Robert Schnase writes about staying awake. His writing is based on Mark 13:33-37, where Jesus three times gives the simple imperative to keep awake. Bishop Schnase writes,

> For Jesus to repeat this so emphatically three times in a row implies that one of the great hazards of the faith journey is spiritual acquiescence, a kind of grogginess that dulls us to what is true, and truly important. Sleepiness of spirit means we miss out on what God is doing, and perhaps overlook the presence of Christ right in our midst. By simply falling asleep, spiritually speaking, we miss God and miss out on what God is calling us to be and do.

He goes on to say,

> If it hadn't been for Mary and company on Easter morning, the disciples would have slept through the resurrection of Christ. In my mind, this also accounts for the person in need of healing who reported, "I see people as trees walking." A dulling of spiritual insight causes us to see people as things and to overlook how each is a child of God.[1]

Again, I say how easy it is to live a church life while being spiritually detached.

This area has been really hard in my life in ministry. There have certainly been seasons of a sense of God's presence of closeness in my life and seasons of desert and loneliness in the perceived absence of God's presence. People have teased me all my

---

1. Robert Schnase, *The Balancing Act: A Daily Rediscovery of Grace* (Nashville: Abingdon, 2009), 35–36.

life that I don't act spiritual or look very spiritual. I don't exude the language of spirituality very much. I have had the experience of gathering up my ordination papers and driving to the district superintendent's office to say I was done with ministry because of the perceived distance of God's presence and the difficulty of ministry.

Most people would perceive my spirituality to be different from what they've come to consider normal spirituality, particularly of a pastor. I'm not sure what "normal" spirituality would look like, though. Still I have been judged by it nearly all of my life, as most people have been judged, especially pastors.

As laity, I (Kay) have come to my own realization around the spirituality "norms" for clergy. I was raised with the perception that pastors had a higher spiritual connection with God, having been called to ministry and attended seminary. At first, it disappointed and discouraged me that the clergy I was working with seemed not to have that higher connection with Christ in the way they lived their lives and ran their churches. The longer I have worked with clergy, the more I have discovered they are more like me than different in our spiritual walks. They, too, have seasons of walking closer to God than they walk in others. They, too, have seasons of walking closer to God than other times in their own faith journey. They, too, struggle with staying spiritually grounded amid day-to-day life. While I had a perception that pastors were taught in seminary how to be spiritual and how to practice spirituality, I have discovered this is not the case for most clergy. Most seminaries teach pastors how to be theologians. Laity also tend to believe pastors are taught how to lead a church as well as how to be spiritual. This is not true most of the time. Like me, they had to figure out how to be spiritual and church leaders on their own.

In writing this book, we (Bob and Kay) have discovered the disconnection of clergy and laity on this subject. Laity have a perception that their pastor has it all together spiritually while clergy have a fear of laity knowing their walk is as fragile as anybody else's. Many clergy are not as authentic around this as they need to be because of the laity's unrealistic perceptions and resulting consequences. "What would happen if they really knew?" wonders the pastor. "Would they follow me as their pastor?" Running a church while being spiritually detached leads to burnout (at the very least) for the pastor. Deeper yet, it leads to an emptiness and a hollowness inside that loses track of God.

If we pastors don't figure this out in our lives and in our pastorates, it will create burnout. Figure it out or burn out! It took me a long time to accept that there was no one way to be spiritual. There is no one set of practices that necessarily leads to spirituality for every pastor or person. Yet you do need to find your set of practices that opens the doorway to a spiritual life. If you want to get wet, you've got to find ways to get into the water. John Wesley understood that all of us had the means of grace—spiritual practices that help us stay connected to God—available for us to receive. He also insisted we ought to consistently put ourselves in the means of grace so we will have a better chance of experiencing God. Understanding Wesley's teachings of the means of grace has been very helpful and meaningful in my own practice of spirituality.

> In the same way the Spirit comes to help our weakness. We don't know what we should pray, but the Spirit himself pleads

our case with unexpressed groans. The one who searches hearts knows how the Spirit thinks, because he pleads for the saints, consistent with God's will. (Romans 8:26-27)

Here are some practices that have helped me find a balancing act when it comes to staying spiritually grounded. The key is finding your own rhythm of spirituality.

- Daily reading of scripture with a devotion

- Daily quiet time

- Prayer time

- Being outside working and in nature

- Physical exercise

- Reading books

- Talking to mentors

- Bible study in a group

- Placing visible reminders of Jesus around in my life

While the above list has helped me find my spiritual rhythm, this may not be what you find helpful. Again, experiment with different practices until you find what works for you. There is no "one" way, but you must find "your" way. Michael Slaughter's book *Momentum for Life* was very helpful to me because of the DRIVE acronym of devotion, readiness, investing, visioning, and eating and exercising. It helped me add a rhythm and pattern for a life of spirituality that best fit my personality and lifestyle.

While this is a book about the nine things effective pastors and leaders do differently, I find it interesting that in many churches there were actually very few organized practices of spirituality in place. Almost every church that I have been in has had the need for me to start Bible studies. They simply didn't exist when I arrived. I have had to add prayer rooms, prayer teams, and individuals to pray during all worship services on Sunday morning in every church I have ever served, and I got some of the hardest pushback on all these things. I have learned to do prayer walks both alone and with groups. While these are church things, they added to my own ability to find spirituality amidst my church work.

If I am left to my own devices and no practices, I will not find myself in the means of grace because I have not availed myself of them. When I don't intentionally practice spirituality, oddly enough I find no spiritual peace. **Without spirituality, I don't have . . . a prayer.** In my thirty-seven years of ministry, I have trouble correlating spirituality with being a good leader. However, I can directly correlate not practicing spirituality on a regular basis with being burned out and not a good leader. You can successfully practice church work while being detached spiritually for a short time, but not for the long haul. Therefore get a prayer and find your spiritual rhythm.

Get Grouped and Grounded

After these things, the Lord commissioned seventy-two others and sent them on ahead in pairs to every city and place he was about to go. (Luke 10:1)

Christian existence is "we" existence. (Tex Sample)

I have never seen an effective leader who was not asking questions and seeking information from other people. Effective pastors have a practice and philosophy of continuous learning and growth from all directions—peers, mentors, and laity. One of the early lessons I learned was from Reverend Harold Dodds, pastor of Country Club UMC in Kansas City, Missouri. Harold knocked on my office door the first weekend of my first full-time new appointment at Randolph Memorial UMC in Kansas City. Harold was in his late fifties while I was twenty-five years old. He walked into my office and stated we needed each other. I asked why! He said he was old and needed some of my new ideas. He said I was young and I needed someone to tell me when not to do something. This was one of the greatest gifts of friendship that I ever received. Until his recent death, we continued that same relationship. Harold also taught me to read books about preaching from well-known preachers. He taught me about the need to read other people's works and to learn from them. He taught me a person didn't need to be alive to be a mentor. Their teaching, through books and other media, lives on to teach generations to come. To this day, I either watch, listen to, or read at least one sermon a week from a well-known preacher. It is invaluable.

It reminds me of the Gospel of Luke's story of Jesus sending seventy-two people out into the mission field. It is interesting that Jesus did not send them out alone. Rather, he sent them out in pairs of two. "Why do you suppose Jesus sent out the disciples two by two? Perhaps he knew the resistance they would encounter and the struggles they would experience. He knew they would need each other's strength and encouragement. Nothing is so desperate as a lonely struggle."[1] When Bishop Schnase is teaching on this scripture he goes on to explain, "Jesus sent them out in pairs so that they would talk each other into bolder ministry: 'I'm praying for you. I'm right here beside you. You can do it. God is with you.' And working together provided accountability: 'I can't believe you did that. What were you thinking? You've got to do less of this and more of that next time.' "

Another gift of my relationship with Harold was our weekly meeting to talk about ministry. He asked me questions about what I was preaching on. He asked me, "Have you ever thought about . . . ?" He gave me hundreds of little hints and best practices on the inside scoop on ministry. Harold taught me such

1. Robert Schnase, *Testing and Reclaiming Your Call to Ministry* (Nashville: Abingdon, 1991), 102–3.

invaluable questions as asking the Pastor-Parish Relations Committee chair, "Who do I need to go visit?" Harold was the first of many of my mentors. My experience of effective leaders has been that they are highly connected. They seek information, ask questions, exchange information, and help one another with accountability.

When Reverend Adam Hamilton and I were both preparing to launch our new churches in 1990 in the Kansas City area, we met every Thursday at the Burger King on Wornall in Kansas City, Missouri. We shared ideas, gut-checked our plans, prayed together, and often followed our conversation with a game of racquetball for exercise. We also called people and drove to new church starts to meet with new church pastors to learn everything we possibly could about how to plant a new church before we planted our new churches. For years after we planted our churches, we continued to call one another weekly asking the same questions, checking on one another and seeking best practices.

These are two examples of effective pastors getting grouped. I don't know any successful "lone ranger" pastors. One of the things I have learned is that I have the power to convene people. Nothing has ever stopped me from gathering two or three people around the table, asking questions and sharing best practices. Even in my current position as Director of Congregational Excellence, I helped form a network of other transformational leaders in the United Methodist Church called Route 122. We gather together annually to share best practices and build our friendship. In my lifetime, I have mentored and been mentored at the same time. My whole life, I have constantly been in contact with multiple people in various positions asking questions and sharing best practices. Not only does this create an environment of learning, but it leads to a great network of colleagues and friends.

The first component developed in the Healthy Church Initiative was the continuous learning communities called PLD (pastoral leadership development). These were groups of eight to ten clergy who gathered eight times over the course of a year for a four-hour session of learning, spiritual formation, food, fellowship, and accountability for action steps. Although in Missouri we had experienced clergy cluster groups for encouragement and support, PLD was a new concept that shared best practices, new learning, and accountability for action steps within the fellowship and support. These were learning groups with a purpose. The early groups came together on their own out of a desire to learn from one another and grow their churches. Effective leaders seek out groups to learn in and from. Nobody is stopping United Methodist clergy from getting together on their own to learn together and share best practices. I have had good experiences in the Large-Church Initiative, church-planting initiatives, transformation initiatives, and so forth. Leaders like to connect with other leaders. Most workshops and seminars are good for inspiration and some application. The really great learning occurs in the hallways of these events just as much as it occurs in the event itself. Effective leaders seek out these learning communities.

If you have to be made to become involved in one of these groups, you are probably in the wrong profession. I have never had a time in my life when I was not in some sort of learning community. I have never had a time in my church when I did not put together a learning community with my lay leadership.

I have never had a time when I was not giving my lay leaders books to read or dragging them off to a workshop, a seminar, or another growing church for learning. Sometimes field trips and the resulting conversation on the ride are worth a thousand words.

Many churches only know what they know. And mostly what laity know is the way they have been doing ministry in their own church. As a matter of fact, this is not the way John and Charles Wesley operated the early Methodist movement. Nor was it the way Francis Asbury operated the early American Methodist movement. As a matter of fact, the way we operate in today's church was not the way Jesus operated in his ministry. Nor was it the way of the church in Acts 2. If you want a clear understanding of the way the original church of Jesus Christ operated, read through the book of Acts and the instruction letter to the Ephesian church. Remember, both were bound by the cultures and times that they existed in. You always have to adapt how to present the truth. Remember there is a difference between the mission of Jesus Christ (which never changes) and the methods (which are always changing) one needs to use to present the gospel of Jesus Christ in the ministries of the church. The only way to change the present practices of church is to go, see, and experience something different and then talk about how it applies to your setting. You have to help your church develop a continuous learning attitude along with practicing it yourself. Otherwise you are doomed to simply repeat what you already know. How is that working for you? If you are not careful, one year's experience of ministry will be repeated thirty-nine times. If a church is not careful, it will repeat the actions of its most successful season over and over and over even if that season of success was thirty years ago, thinking, "If we just try harder, surely it will become effective again."

I didn't start out to be a continuous learner. This is a practice I have developed out of the pure desire and need to figure stuff out (and sometimes out of desperation). I have found you don't have a choice of being a continuous learner if you want to be effective in your ministry. Reading is not really my thing, yet I read at least a book a month to stay on top of stuff and not stagnate.

In my work as a new-church-plant supervisor for the last eight years in the UMC's Missouri Annual Conference and through my work with the Healthy Church Initiative, **coaching has become an obvious and essential tool for effective pastors**. I did not experience coaching in the church world prior to 2005. I did experience coaching in football during my time attending Sherwood High School in Creighton, Missouri. This was as the first time anyone had suggested to me that I would become a United Methodist pastor. I laughed at him because at that time in my life that was not conceivable whatsoever. But he saw it. What that taught me was that coaches see things that others don't see. Coaches can sometimes identify gifts you have before you even know you have them. Coaches push you when you don't want to be pushed. Coaches hold you accountable for outcomes. In the church world, coaches ask the invaluable questions that allow you to close the gap between your current reality and where you want to be in your personal ministry and in your church.

My first church coaching experience was in 2005 with Dr. David Hyatt. I was at Church of the Shepherd in St. Peters, Missouri. Our congregation had grown in worship attendance from

600 to 800, which was significantly impacting how we practiced ministry. It significantly challenged the alignment and roles of staff, pastors, and laity. We were desperately trying to figure out why things were not working as well as they had been working just one year earlier. So we turned to a coach. Coaching allowed the opportunity for a time set aside for big-picture dreaming, planning, and conversations. It dawned on me that every day I served as the lead pastor for Church of the Shepherd, I was serving the largest church I had ever served. Each year the church was bigger and each year I found myself serving at a level I did not know and was not prepared for through my seminary or on-the-job training. I was trying to figure out how to pastor the largest church I had ever been a part of and it was growing every day. At the time, I did not have an understanding of what some call "church by size." In other words, depending on the size of your church, you have to practice your ministry differently or you will grow your church down to the previous size church you served effectively. Unless you develop a keen sense of wanting to learn new practices and wanting to be coached to a different level, you are destined to repeat what you know, which will often lead to a declining congregation.

Leaders seek outside voices, people to stretch them and help them develop new practices to take them to next level. As a new-church-plant supervisor, I often look back over the forty-five plants in the state of Missouri over thirty years and wonder why some plants made it and others did not. It has become obvious to me that the number one trait of those that made it was their coachability. Those that didn't grow large enough to become a viable congregation were oftentimes led by pastors who did not or would not accept being coached. Many times pastors lacked the self-awareness that they needed coaching, that coaching could be beneficial and/or that coaching could be helpful in increasing their effectiveness. What I mean by self-awareness is that we clearly need to understand that each of us has limits in our capabilities. We have our own personal blind spots. Each of us has need of an understanding of our strengths and weaknesses and needs to be open to the possibility of growth, shifts, and new practices.

Effective leaders are self-aware! They are aware of who they are and who they are not. They are aware of where they are and where they are not. In my experience supervising UMC pastors who are not very effective, I have found that they lack this self-awareness. Without self-awareness, it is very hard to be coachable.

As you continue to grow as a leader, you need to grow in your confidence. Leadership requires confidence. However, confidence without humility leads to arrogance and is off-putting to most people. Leadership requires a dosage of humility and self-reflection. Without those you can know a lot and come off as very condescending. You may be right, but you are certainly not going to be heard, respected, or followed. On the other hand, when leaders are not as competent in their skill set as they need to be, sometimes they try to overcompensate and come off as defensive and cannot hear new ideas, learnings, and possibilities. If you have a strong personality, you have a far greater risk of coming across as arrogant. I know this by experience. I have led my whole life with confidence, though I am not quite sure where it came from other than a natural inheritance. I certainly did not get it from my original academic abilities. Sometimes my confidence is interpreted as arrogance. Sometimes my boldness has been interpreted as pushiness. I have had to learn when to dial it back and to add a dose of humor, compassion, and patience. Humility with confidence is a balancing act that is worth the risk to attempt as you put yourself out there in leadership. Confident leaders must be open to fierce feedback and learning. If one is not open to fierce feedback, one might be bordering on arrogance. Less competent leaders must be open to learning, growing, and feedback without being defensive.

We need confident, competent leaders in the church! We do not need arrogant leaders in the church. We do not need more nonreflective leaders or leaders lacking self-awareness in the church. I am sure that the Apostle Paul sometimes struggled with his balance of confidence and arrogance. But it was worth the risk. For without Paul, where would the church of the New Testament be today? Paul was a confident leader. Today, we have learned that confident leaders are not afraid to be coached, to be in a continuous learning group, to have a mentor, and to be in continuous modes of connection, questioning, and seeking best practices.

Speak the Truth with Determined Patience

*Then you will know the truth, and the truth will set you free.
(John 8:32)*

*However, when the Spirit of truth comes, he will guide you in
all truth. He won't speak on his own, but will say whatever he
hears and will proclaim to you what is to come. (John 16:13)*

Make them holy in the truth; your word is truth. (John 17:17)

Speak truth to power. (Baynard Rustin)

*I thought, I'll forget him; I'll no longer speak in his name.
But there's an intense fire in my heart, trapped in my bones.
(Jeremiah 20:9)*

For my entire life, people have said I am plain-spoken.
One could take this a number of ways. Sometimes people
mean I have been too forthcoming and too blunt. Other
times people value it as being transparent, open, honest, and
straightforward. Many times it has served me well. Other times,

45

not so much. I have not served a church where truth-telling was not a necessity in helping the church find its effectiveness. I have never supervised staff (paid or unpaid) without moments when truth-telling was a critical tool required. There have just been so many times in the life of the church and ministry when the niceness culture was so embedded that people were unable to actually speak the truth.

But I have to admit that being the one to burst the bubble of the niceness culture through my straightforwardness often caused just as much pain for me as it did for those who received it. We are so accustomed in the church to not telling it like it is. When we don't tell the truth, we risk a conflict-adverse culture within the church with both laity and clergy. It has led us to be unable to deal with conflict in a healthy manner. Rather, we just avoid conflict at all cost. Somehow we have come up with the idea that being nice is equivalent to being Christian, as though speaking truth (especially if painful) is not being Christian. If you look at Jesus's life, there are certainly two sides to the Savior. There is the sweet side with all the nice sayings of Jesus that we love to memorize at vacation Bible school and sing about, too. Then there is the other side of Jesus, which I often refer to as the hard sayings of Jesus. Jesus spoke the truth very sharply at times, very directly at times. In John's Gospel, he speaks of the "truth" repeatedly. Over two hundred times in the Bible, truth is mentioned. Yet in our niceness culture of the church, if you speak the truth, even in love, you will be both admired and unappreciated. If you only speak the truth without grace, you will simply not be heard.

Cautionary Note: Truth-telling has to be managed well or it hurts people—both the receiver and you. Truth-telling, in love, has to be done at appropriate moments and in measured ways. I have had to learn to lead more with grace so that when truth-telling is required, people have a better chance to receive it and receive it well. Leading with grace in most of your ministry helps people be more open to hearing the moments of truth-telling. On the other hand, if you never truth-tell, the real issues of a congregation or an individual will rarely be admitted or solved. I have encountered many situations in the church and with personnel where there is a laundry list of issues that need to be addressed. It is a laundry list because previous pastors and leaders have been unwilling or unable to address the issues truthfully and/or timely. However, to address them all at once would be overwhelming in the situation or with the person and could lead to a detrimental result or outcome. We tend to value our relationships with one another over achieving the mission. Therefore, we lose the very mission we aspire to accomplish. On the other hand, if we only value the mission without regard for relationships, you will lose the chance of accomplishing the mission. **Timing and the dosage is everything.** But it still must be done if you want to move the church forward. I have had to learn over the course of my ministry to be very careful with truth-telling. What seems to me to be very normal conversation can feel like criticism and harshness when you are living in the niceness culture. The ability to speak the truth in love is absolutely fundamental if you are going to have a ministry of effectiveness. You cannot be held hostage by the culture of niceness. **Niceness does not always lead to faithfulness or effectiveness.**

There is a balancing in ministry between being patient and being confrontational. I often refer to this as "determined patience." If all you have in ministry is compassion and patience, you will be a really nice pastor, but it will be difficult in today's church to be effective. On the other hand, if you are only confrontational, you will alienate the very people you are trying to get to follow you. Again, in today's church it will be very difficult to be effective. It is a bit of an art form to read the landscape so that you, as a leader, might know when to push, when to confront, when to back off, when to encourage, and when to be patient. *M.A.S.H.* is one of my favorite shows. Radar O'Reilly knew how to read a room very well. He had a kind of sixth sense that allowed him to quickly identify the mood of the group, the key influencers in the group, and the next steps that might need to be taken. We could all learn something from Radar. Reading the room takes a good dose of intuition and common sense. It is like walking a tightrope. You could easily fall off the rope on either side, and I have done this multiple times in my ministry. Yet you have to walk out onto the tightrope if you want effectiveness in your ministry. When you fall off (and you will), you get up, apologize, course-correct, and try again.

What has built trustworthiness for me in my ministry is not just my plain-spokenness, but also my ability to apologize and course-correct when I get it wrong. What helps create transparency is when you make a mistake and are willing to be open, accept blame, take responsibility, correct course, and apologize. There have been multiple times in my ministry when things have not gone right. I often put the people around a table to talk about what is going on and say, "Let's be open and honest about this and figure out what we need to do." It is this kind of atmosphere that builds trust and makes people relatable. Most people think they can come in and talk to me, even though they may not like what I tell them. The key here is being very consistent and promote open communication at all levels! This whole paragraph describes the ingredients of what some might refer to as being authentic. Authenticity is particularly important to the millennial generation. If the church is going to reach a new, younger generation of people, we have to let go of the pretending and stop holding a niceness culture above being authentic and transparent. It is this very reason that millennials think Christians are hypocritical. I am not suggesting we can't be nice, but I am suggesting we ought to be real. This really is breaking the mold of how church has been done in the past.

You could be the best tightrope walker in the world balancing patience and determination, but if you do not also wrap this in an overall attitude of enthusiasm, encouragement, and general optimism for the future, it will not work. Remember, in chapter 1 we started with enthusiasm. You cannot lose enthusiasm or you will be unable to move through the difficult issues that need to be worked on in ministry. Remember, we just said most of your ministry should be led with grace. The ability to be an encourager and see possibilities in people is essential for effective ministry. You must have the skill of being an encourager in the midst of being a truth-teller. You must have a mix of being able to see the potential in people and giving them enough time to realize and live into that potential while along the way being as straightforward and truthful as possible.

You have to have enough confidence to be permission-giving to people and enough confidence not to micromanage people. Pastors, you do not have to be in control of everything. You do need to be in control of some things. In fact, being in control of everything is not healthy for you or the congregation. Likewise, being in control of nothing is not healthy for you or the congregation. It is important to stay focused on the right things and not get distracted by the urgent. It is important to let other people be in charge and run ministries. It is important, as a truth-teller, to give people honest, constructive feedback. Truth-telling with patience allows people to know their blind spots and grow. Once again you are walking the tightrope between overfunctioning as a pastor and underfunctioning as a pastor.

Pastors, if you are going to lead, you are going to bleed. Lead smart! If you lead smart, you will have bumps, bruises, and scratches, but you won't bleed to death or bleed on others. You will not hurt as many people if you lead smart. If you are a leader, there are going to be times in your ministry when your leadership leaves some people in your wake. We all have regrets and wish for do-overs because we didn't lead as smartly as we could have and ended up hurting people. I have done it. I did it early on in my ministry more than I do it today. I have learned to be a better tightrope walker and learned to be a better truth-teller with grace. It is an acquired skill set and necessary if you are going to be an effective pastor. Yet I will not be held hostage today by a fear of making a mistake in my attempts to be authentic, effective, and true. And neither should you as a pastor. The church needs more truth-tellers. But remember to start with grace. We are United Methodists. We lead with grace, then truth, but it is not just grace and not just truth. Nor is it truth with no grace. **It is grace and then truth.** So step up . . . carefully and with determined patience. You just might be amazed at the effectiveness of your ministry when it includes both grace and truth.

Chapter Seven

Lead Up and
Manage Down

Now when the Human One comes in his majesty and all his angels are with him, he will sit on his majestic throne. All the nations will be gathered in front of him. He will separate them from each other, just as a shepherd separates the sheep from the goats. He will put the sheep on his right side. But the goats he will put on his left. (Matthew 25:31-33)

You are the salt of the earth. But if salt loses its saltiness, how will it become salty again? It's good for nothing except to be thrown away and trampled under people's feet. (Matthew 5:13)

Jesus returned from the Jordan River full of the Holy Spirit, and was led by the Spirit into the wilderness. There he was tempted for forty days by the devil. He ate nothing during those days and afterward Jesus was starving. The devil said to him, "Since you are God's Son . . ." (Luke 4:1-3)

I won't accept bulls from your house. (Psalm 50:9)

51

The art of self-leadership is essential and foundational. If you do not develop the art of self-leadership, it is very hard to imagine you will develop other leaders. In the introduction, we asked the question of whether leadership was a trait you could develop or something you were born with. Our answer was yes. It is both. It is both your personality and a learned behavior. The first step in leadership is the leadership of self. There are some really great tools to learn about yourself and your leadership style. These tools includes such things as the DiSC profile, StrengthsFinder, Myers Briggs, 360 Evaluations, and any number of other tools. Each profile measures a different aspect of your personality or your skill set. So each offers a unique picture of your own leadership and personality. Effective pastors know their leadership gifts and challenges. If you are unsure about your leadership gifts and challenges, it is critical for you to gain knowledge to help grow your leadership abilities and a greater self-awareness. This is also where coaching can be very helpful.

Levels of Leadership:

1. Self
2. Leading another
3. Leading a team
4. Leading an organization
5. Leading leaders
6. Leading a network
7. Leading the world

Take a look at the list above. What leadership level have you achieved? Where do you need to invest and learn more skills? What could allow you to take your leadership skills to the next level?

After thirty-seven years of ministry, I still remember hiring my first secretary at the church in Celeste, Texas. The position was part-time and the first time I had hired someone in the life of a church. It is the first time I had a paid staff person. I did not have a clue as to what I was doing. I think we hired a friend of a friend, which is what often happens in the life of the church. I got lucky and it worked out. Looking back, it is pretty obvious that I had not mastered the skill of leading another. As I look back, I remember the first time I led a team, the first time I led a larger organization, the first time I led leaders, and only recently the first time I led a network of leaders. I would have to confess that most of the time, I learned how to lead on the job ("OJT"). That is the hard way to learn leadership. It might have been better had someone told me early on that I was going to need to learn the art of leadership. Many times pastors have been thrown into the third or fourth level of leadership without having the skills and experience for leading being beyond a first- or second-level leader. A great many of our pastors today grew up in smaller, declining congregations and have not experienced leadership in large, growing congregations. Sometimes our second-career pastors have an advantage because they have had a secular job in a larger organization where they had training and experience in leadership. Most seminaries are equipped to produce theologians, not necessarily leaders. Most pastors entered the ministry thinking they were going to be shepherds and theologians and now are being called upon to be shepherd leaders. I have trouble thinking of a single effective pastor who has not figured out the majority of the levels of leadership. Friends, go get whatever help you need to be a successful shepherd leader. **It is all about leadership . . . self, others, and organization.**

Besides developing your own leadership skills, you and your church need to have an intentional plan for identifying the next generation of leaders. It is important for pastors to invest time in your leaders—current and future. Effective pastors have an intentional, teaching plan to equip leaders in their congregations. Twenty-first-century church leadership is not the same as the leadership most of our laity learned growing up in the church. It requires attention and time to teach competent, secular leaders how to lead in the twenty-first-century church. This does not happen by osmosis or through referring to your pictorial directory once a year and asking people to join some committee promising it won't take any time or commitment at all. Friends, leadership in the twenty-first-century church takes time, commitment, and intentionality to be effective. We have to quit acting like it doesn't matter who our leaders are. These are no longer considered positions of honor but rather are positions of leadership that bear the responsibility of effectiveness in their congregations.

It is important to understand "church by size." Every pastor serves a congregation of a certain size. Most church consultants consider there to be six different church sizes. While different models suggest different size breaks, it is important to notice how the role of the pastor changes with the size of the worshipping congregation.

- Very Small: Family chapel, pastor-centered pastoral role, under 50 people in worship

- Small: Shepherd-pastor pastoral role, under 100 people in worship

- Mid-Size: Program-driven, leader-shepherd pastoral role, 100–350 people in worship

- Large: Corporate, leader-shepherd pastoral role, 350–750 people in worship

- Very Large: Corporate, leader-preacher as pastoral role, 750–1,500 people in worship

- Mega Church: Movement leader, over 1,500 in worship attendance

Every consultant may have her or his own way of listing and naming the various church sizes, but we must understand the different leadership needed for the various sizes. We call this concept "church by size." At each size of church, how one practices ministry is different and must be different or the church will shrink back to the size of ministry you are practicing. Effective pastors have had to learn the nuances and differences among the sizes of churches and how their roles change at each size. No size is good or bad. Rather, size makes a difference in how one leads and practices ministry. It is important to understand this concept because it will affect how you lead up and how you manage down in your ministry. By leading up, we mean knowing where to invest your time and energy, recognizing where they will be effective. By managing down, we mean knowing where *not* to spend your time and energy, recognizing where ministry is not effective. Each spring, many bushes need their dead limbs pruned to allow for new growth. We need to fertilize and weed the areas where abundance is most possible and not tend to the parts that are no longer effective or bearing fruit.

The following scripture explains there are seasons for everything. We must clearly evaluate if we are in a season of leading up or managing down in each area of our ministry.

Ecclesiastes 3:1-8

There's a season for everything
and a time for every matter under the heavens:
a time for giving birth and a time for dying,
a time for planting and a time for uprooting what was planted,
a time for killing and a time for healing,
a time for tearing down and a time for building up,
a time for crying and a time for laughing,
a time for mourning and a time for dancing,
a time for throwing stones and a time for gathering stones,
a time for embracing and a time for avoiding embraces,
a time for searching and a time for losing,
a time for keeping and a time for throwing away,
a time for tearing and a time for repairing,
a time for keeping silent and a time for speaking,
a time for loving and a time for hating,
a time for war and a time for peace.

Leading up and managing down has first to do with yourself and then with leading your followers. Leading up and managing down also has to do with determining what is important, fruit-bearing, and effective in your ministry setting and what is not. It is knowing where to invest your time and energy and where not to invest. What ministries do you feed? What ministries do you starve? What priorities do you lift up? What priorities do you let go? Who do you pour into? Who do you not let distract you? What voices do you listen to? What voices do you not listen to? There will always be lots of voices around you as a pastor. Some of those voices will be very loud and consistent. Some will be soft-spoken on the fringes of your church and hard to hear. Some of those voices might be outside in the mission field that have yet to be heard. Sorting out priorities is a huge task. When we do not prioritize purposefully and prayerfully, we will be faced with a church that is going a hundred different directions at one time. Every direction is important to somebody and at one time did very good work and may still. But this may not be where your church needs to focus today or in the future. We cannot be held hostage by the fear of offending somebody because the church is no longer going to invest in his or her particular ministry. Too often we save a particular ministry, but we lose track of the mission for fear of offending somebody (relationships over mission). The gift of discernment is essential if a pastor and congregation are to be effective. If you are not careful your church will be an inch deep and a mile wide in your attempt to be something for everybody while not being anything significant for anybody.

Learning what to ignore and what to tackle with your time and energy will be essential if effectiveness is to occur. If you, with your lay leadership, can set a clear direction while understanding your mission field, knowing your congregation's affinity and ability, knowing your own affinity, and praying for God's call upon the congregation, this will facilitate the process of recognizing what to tackle and what to ignore. One of the traits of effective pastors and congregations is the ability to discern all of this together. This allows you to develop a plan and then work the plan. I do not know any growing congregation that is not working a plan of some sort. No plan equates to no effectiveness. I grew up in a small farming town of three hundred people. We had a garden. You were unable to plant seed without a plan for the garden. If you simply went to the garden and threw out a bunch of seeds hoping for something to happen, all you got was a mess of weeds and no fruits or vegetables. It takes a plan. Most plans today are not more than eighteen months at best. I do not believe in long-range planning (more than two years), because of the fast-paced, ever-changing world we live in today. But I do believe in short-range planning. Plans are always fluid and flexible. They are not set in concrete. How many times have we gone to churches or sat down with pastors and asked about their plan for the next week, for the next month, for the next three months, for the next six months, and for the next eighteen months? Rarely is there such a plan. What is your plan?

Communicate, communicate, communicate! It is impossible to overcommunicate in our social-media world of today. How many good plans have we seen go up in smoke because we stumbled with the rollout and the communication with the congregation for buy-in? There is no plan without communication. You cannot lead without being a good communicator. I still think Andy Stanley and Lane Jones's *Communicating for a Change* is one of the best communication books for church leadership to read. Knowing where to focus, how to lead up, how to manage down, how to lead across, what to take up, and what to leave behind is essential in pastoral leadership of an effective congregation. None of it happens without a plan and without communicating. So get a plan and communicate it over and over and over. Remember, just communicating "what" we want to do is likely to not convince people to move forward. We have to first communicate the "why." The "why" provides more opportunity to convince people to move forward. The "why" connects to the mission.

Many times churches are running what we refer to as a spoke-and-hub operation. A spoke-and-hub operation is where a pastor is at the center of everything that happens. For example: laity, if you have the perception that the pastor must be at every meeting and every hospital visit, you are running a spoke-and-hub operation. If the pastor is not involved or causing something to happen, then more than likely it does not happen.

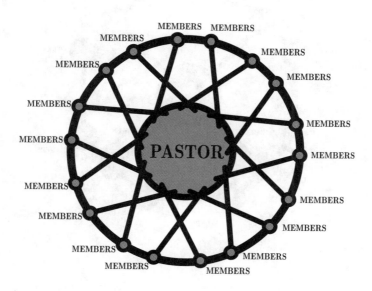

Spoke-and-Hub Operation

If the church is functioning as a spoke-and-hub operation, communication can be tricky. This is especially true if the pastor is not the best communicator. If nothing happens until it goes through the wheel, also known as the pastor, then it would also be true that communication does not happen until it starts with the pastor. Communication will most likely be an issue, since everything runs through the pastor. On the other side: pastor, if good, effective communication does not come naturally to you, you will need to put some systems, processes, and people in place to help you.

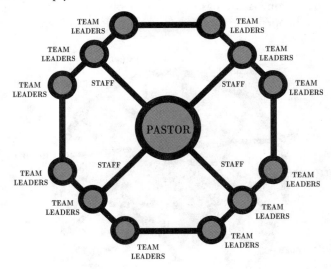

Pastor Leader System

For churches to grow beyond the family-size church of fifty people in worship attendance, the church must move beyond the spoke-and-hub operation. The pastor needs to be leading the church to accomplish the mission and vision, but ministry can (and should) happen without the pastor's direct involvement each and every moment. The larger the church grows, the more the pastor needs to be involved in identifying and equipping leaders rather than leading and implementing every ministry. Remember, **a church can only grow at the rate that the number and depth of leaders develop.**

Communication methods and processes must change as a church grows. Communication does not occur the same way in a family-sized church as it does in a programmatic or corporate-sized church. In order to communicate correctly and effectively, one must take church size into consideration. We oftentimes find that churches are still trying to communicate as if they are at least one size smaller than they truly are. As the church was growing, their communication methods did not grow in parallel to accommodate church size. Consider investing in learning and studying the church one size larger than you are now so that you are ready and able to grow into the next-largest size of church. If you don't, you may very well limit your growth potential because the church will be unable to communicate effectively for its new size. One way some of us trip up in communicating is by evaluating our church size by the one worship service we attend (if multiple services are offered) rather than by all the worship services combined or the overall membership. Whatever the size of your church, you must always be paying attention to communication. If your church is growing, you need to be communicating as though you are one size larger than you are. Otherwise, communication will hinder your ability to grow.

In most every consultation we conduct, communication is cited as a problem. Sometimes "communication problems" are a big bucket of lots of different issues that all get combined together and labeled as "communication problems." But most times, there are some real communication gaps. Remember, you must find relevant methods to communicate as the pastor as well as methods for your leaders and congregation to communicate effectively. We must also continuously evaluate not only the effectiveness but the methods themselves. As new means of communication are invented or made available, we must be ready to embrace them for the sake of reaching new people or those who appreciate and invest in the latest technology.

Communication takes many forms. Communication must be repeated to first be heard and then subsequently be comprehended. As a leader, you have most often thought or talked about an idea or event for quite some time before it ever becomes public. So what feels like old news to you is brand new information to others. Do not allow your own feeling of "knowing" information to be your barometer for others' comprehension and understanding of information. Just about the time you feel you have communicated sufficiently is when people are just beginning to hear the information or message. So communicate, communicate, and communicate in various places, in various ways, with various people! It is essential to good leadership!

Chapter Eight

Preach and Worship Well

Peter stood with the other eleven apostles. He raised his voice and declared, "Judeans and everyone living in Jerusalem! Know this! Listen carefully to my words!" (Acts 2:14)

He stayed with the disciples in Damascus for several days. Right away, he began to preach about Jesus in the synagogues. "He is God's Son," he declared.
Everyone who heard him was baffled. They questioned each other, "Isn't he the one who was wreaking havoc among those in Jerusalem who called on this name? Hadn't he come here to take those same people as prisoners to the chief priests?"
But Saul grew stronger and stronger. He confused the Jews who lived in Damascus by proving that Jesus is the Christ. (Acts 9:19b-22)

Praise seeking understanding. (Jason Byassee)

Good preaching covers a multitude of sins—yours and theirs! In other words, it is hard to bring transformation and effectiveness to any church without good preaching. Good preaching lets you bring about change. If you preach change, you can get some change. If you don't preach well, it is hard to get any change. You can preach your way into people's hearts. Preaching is to worship what worship is to the rest of the church. If worship goes well, so go the rest of the ministries in the church. If worship is lackluster, boring, and not compelling, it is hard to imagine the ministries of the church being any different the rest of the week. Likewise, it is hard to imagine exciting worship with lackluster preaching. It is incredibly hard to pull off an exciting, spirited sermon if the rest of the worship experience is lackluster, so these two are connected. We have all experienced worship services with flashes of excellence and moments of mediocrity all within the same hour. We have also all experienced sermons with the same combination. I hate to be harsh here, but in practicing my truth-telling, I have to say the church is dying for good preaching. I am not hung up on any particular style for preaching or worship, but we have to do both with excellence, and they must be compelling. I do not know a church that is growing without good preaching. Now there are churches with good preaching that are not growing, but good preaching is a must to be a growing, vibrant congregation that is effective.

In my opinion good preaching revolves around these elements:

- The ability to connect with the congregation—verbally and nonverbally

- The art of good storytelling

- The use of humor in an appropriate manner

- The use of visuals/multimedia/social media

- Biblically based with some depth

- One-third information and two-thirds application to life

- Liveliness

- A unified theme

In seminary I was taught that sermon preparation began with spending hours in the scripture and hours in the commentaries, writing a manuscript, reducing it to an outline, memorizing it, and then finally delivering it without notes. The manuscript would include three points to help the congregation reflect on the topic and lead them to their own conclusions. The sermon was more of a history lesson and a biblical study. It did not include application.

Here is how I put together a sermon today and what I teach others in my preaching workshop:

1. Determine your goal: What do you expect someone in the congregation to go do?

2. Pick a point: Reduce it to one word. Have a purpose/outcome you are hoping for. What's the one thing?

3. Create a map: This could include a story, image, video, drama, and liturgy.

4. Internalize the message: How does it relate to me, you, and scripture?

5. My story

6. Your story

7. Scripture story

8. How do we go forward together?

9. Engage your audience: Speak to real life. Remember they have an eight-minute attention span. This is about inspiration and motivation more than learning. Learning is done in Bible studies and other weekday opportunities.

10. Find your voice: Share your real experiences without bleeding on your congregation.

11. Start all over.

This is simply my method of getting an effective, compelling sermon together. You need to find your way. No two people are the same in how they do sermon prep. I prefer to do sermon series, but again this will be cultural and has varied over my thirty-seven years in ministry. Sometimes I have used the lectionary. Sometimes I have been a topical preacher. But most of the last fifteen years I have done sermon series. I think sermon series give the congregation a place to start and stop. It gives a reason to invite. It allows worship arts and music people to have a theme over a number of weeks. It allows you to focus and go deeper during those weeks and yet not be too deep on any one week. Do not assume that people know the biblical story. Do not use too much church language. There is a lot of value in looking at your sermon and worship experience through the lens of all the senses (see it, hear it, write it, smell it, feel it).

I have not written a sermon by myself in years while serving a local church. Using a creative worship-planning team is very helpful. I think it is almost imperative in today's multimedia culture. It takes more than one person to come up with ideas and come up with the connections to the culture. This is a team effort! You are looking for the felt need in the culture and a way to connect biblically to it. Reading books, going to movies, plays, and dramas, and hanging out at Starbucks all help you connect with the culture. There is no need to start from scratch when there is so much great material already out there in terms of resources produced by other pastors or churches and through the culture itself (such as YouTube, blogs, focus groups, news feeds, Google, and so forth). The creative worship team should look for music and a centerpiece (one word) for the day and search the scriptures for appropriate connections. The creative worship team does things like making a mock-up of the worship order for the series, helping with sermon possibilities, brainstorming for the visuals needed to help carry out the theme, and so on. With a worship-planning team I didn't come up with ideas and themes myself. Each team member was given homework to research in order to bring back their own suggestions for sermon series.

The creative worship team was a lot of fun for me as a pastor. This team kept me from being a lone ranger preacher trying to come up with a new idea every seven days. Every seven days comes pretty often when you have to do it by yourself. The process and end result are much better when you aren't doing it by yourself. Some pastors are hesitant to work with a worship team because it feels like it will take more time and be yet another thing to do. For me, it actually lifted the burden and spread the work around. As a result it led to a much better outcome in the quality and relevance of both the sermon and the overall worship service.

For me, the creative worship team involved between three to six people meeting weekly with a monthly day-long retreat used for planning. A bigger team (12–20 people) gathered for a quarterly retreat for brainstorming. It was not always the same people. The size of your team is dependent on the size of your church. The weekly group was working on the coming Sunday. The monthly group was working on the current series. The quarterly group was working on two or three series at once for the next quarter's series. We did a dress rehearsal for every worship service on the Saturday before the Sunday worship. The creative worship team's job was to create a cohesive worship experience that fit with the sermon so well that by the time I got up to preach, everybody already knew what the topic was for that day. That's like receiving the football on the one-yard line before calling the play to go into the end zone. Many times in churches I find the opposite occurring: the preacher receives the ball on the opposite end of the field and has to drive all the way down the field for a touchdown.

Anybody participating in worship was expected to be at rehearsal. I think this is crucial, but I find very few clergy or lay people willing to do it. You only have the one hour of Sunday once (or whatever the day and time is for your main worship service). You get my point. Worship and preaching is the deal!

Preaching and worship is so important. Yet when I drive around and visit congregations on Sunday morning, I am continually astounded at how poorly we do worship and preaching. This is not because people are not trying hard. It is not because preachers are not putting in preparation time. But for some reason, worship is still not very compelling or competent and lacks sustenance. The art of lively preaching seems to be lost. Now this is very personal. I may have already offended most of our present preachers. My experience is that every preacher thinks he or she is a good preacher. But friends, it is time to get real and to get better. We CAN do this better. First you find a trusted mentor, someone who ACTUALLY is a gifted preacher, to give you honest feedback. Oftentimes, videotaping yourself and viewing it with your mentor is very helpful. This is one of the ways I learned to be a preacher. Read Adam Hamilton's excellent brief book *Speaking Well*, and reread it each year. Other helpful hints for me were to watch gifted preachers, read sermons, go to movies looking for contemporary themes to connect with the culture, listen to storytellers, and take a number of speech classes. Dress-rehearse your sermon. Watch stand-up comic routines—comedians have to connect with an audience or they bomb the routine. Do whatever it takes to get better. And always continue to get better. Invest in whatever resources it takes to get better. This investment in preaching and worship experience will change the trajectory of a pastoral ministry more than anything else will.

Have Some Fun

*I am shocked at how many people are bothered by children and
student ministries* having fun.
*You can measure the temperature of a church by how much its
people* laugh.
Joy *attracts people.*
*Until you are having fun with a child, they're not sure if you
like them.*
We were made to have fun. *(Reggie Joiner, at Orange Conference 2013)*

*So I commend enjoyment because there's nothing better for
people to do under the sun but to eat, drink, and be glad. This
is what will accompany them in their hard work, during the
lifetime that God gives under the sun. (Ecclesiastes 8:15)*

*Yes, you will go out with celebration, and you will be brought
back in peace. Even the mountains and the hills will burst into
song before you. (Isaiah 55:12)*

I have yet to find a church that is growing that is not having
fun. This may be the most underrated element of church-
growth strategy in the world. Reggie Joiner is right. At the

Orange Conference in 2013 Joiner stated, "*Joy* attracts people" and "You can measure the temperature of a church by how much its people *laugh*."[1] People have so much negativity and stress going on in their everyday lives that they certainly don't need more of it at the church. It is impossible to have a completely stress-free environment. Any time you put a group of people together, it takes a great deal of work to make it work. The Bible says that where two or three or gathered, so is the presence of God. I say where two or three are gathered, you better hope there is the presence of God because you are going to need it. In light of that, you need to strategically plan some fun—both inside and outside the church. Church work is hard! Jesus had hard days to say the least. It may not be a mistake that Jesus's first miracle was turning water into wine at a wedding to make sure the wedding party had a good time (and to make his mother happy). Jesus is found many times hanging out with people and in places that you would not expect. I wonder if he was not simply having a good time, because we know he spent many other days/hours in prayer, teaching, performing miracles, answering questions, and moving from place to place. We know he had times of confrontation, truth-telling, explaining, and trying to keep the disciples straight, and we know he practiced going up to the synagogue. But he also practiced going to dinner, throwing parties, and hanging out with people you would least expect. Likewise a pastor and church need to have some fun!

We need to debunk the idea that the church has to be a stuffy place—a place where only "religious" people go or a place that is boring and always so very serious. I think hanging around

1. As quoted by Elle Campbell, "3 Reasons Your Ministry Needs to Have More Fun!," *ElleCampbell.org* (May 20, 2013), http://ellecampbell.org/have-more-fun/.

Jesus might have been quite interesting—at times even fun. At other times, hanging around with Jesus might have been scary and downright frightening. Wouldn't it be something if when you went to church, you just were not sure what would happen? I understand that the church needs to be a safe place and a place that I can just go and be. But I also think the church can be a place that is both challenging and unpredictable. Boring and status quo is probably not what Jesus intended church to be. I think there needs to be some tension—the joy and enjoyment of Jesus and the challenge and seriousness of Jesus. I have been to some nondenominational churches where the leaders announced we were just going to enjoy God that day in worship. That was surprising to me at first. I had never heard that phrase in my United Methodist churches. But the longer I have been in ministry the more I just want to stand up on Sunday and scream, "Let's just enjoy God today and the company of each other!"

As a pastor, I work hard. I also play hard. I do think you ought to work hard. But I also think you need to take your day off. I have a deep belief that I do not ask lay people to do what I have not already done or what I am unwilling to do. But I also have a deep belief in taking sabbatical—taking time apart and enjoying the company of good friends, good food, good drink, and a good cigar. I believe Wesley taught us this value of moderation.

Most people told me early on in my ministry that as a pastor you should never invest too deeply in the laity of your church as friends because some day you will have to move. When you move, you will need to have complete separation from that family of faith so the new pastor can become their pastor. But I have found deep friendships in my congregations and think you must invest in those friendships if you are to be effective in ministry. On the other hand, when I first started a district superintendent told me that my best friends would be other clergy, which I thought was ridiculous. Thirty-five years later, it turns out to be true. While I have deep friendships within each of the congregations I have served, they were for a season of my life. I would not trade them for anything. But, the truth is, as pastor you move on to the next mission field when you move. You must move on! Don't go back! If you do go back, you will get in the way of the pastor following you. It will also hinder you from making new relationships deeply in your current congregation. I don't cut off people from my previous churches, but my level of friendship and involvement changes dramatically. Quite frankly, I have never understood how you could have time to go back if you are honestly working your new mission field. This is yet another tightrope walk. It is easy as a pastor who invests deeply in friendships to get outside of the boundaries that the office of the pastor necessarily requires. I made that mistake in my new church plant by becoming deep friends with the core group of leaders. I was their friend who happened to be their pastor, so that when I made some difficult decisions regarding the life of the congregation, these same friends thought I had turned on them. "How could I choose the role of being pastor over the role of being their friend?" This was my error. It hurt them and it hurt me forever. I learned you need to be the pastor who happens to be their friend. Today, my best friends turn out to be other clergy. This does not mean I don't invest in relationships with people in the congregations I lead and have some fun. I just have to be their pastor first and their friend second.

When you have staff (paid and unpaid), you must invest time in "leading up" your staff through learnings, spiritual development, and relationship-building. Do you have time planned for fun with your staff? The bigger the church you serve, the more time you need to spend with your paid staff. They are an extension of your office. How they do in their ministries is how you are going to do in your ministry. What kind of time are you investing in your staff?

Effective pastors build fun into their routine. They build fun into the routine of the church. A good dose of humor goes a long way to showing some humility. A good dose of humor keeps you and everybody else from taking you and others too seriously. The ability to show your real self is essential. Your congregation needs to see your humanness, too. What better way to show it than by having fun with your congregation? I have had some of my best experiences playing softball, going on canoe trips, camping, taking mission trips, building houses, mowing the church lawn, and taking part in church clean-up days, vacation Bible school, and parties. These kinds of activities are life- and relationship-builders. There is nothing better than riding motorcycles with someone from church, talking sports cars, or going to a football or baseball game. These all help you as the pastor make connections and be a "real" person. Do you have fun times built into your church calendar? Do you have fun times built into your personal calendar for you and your family?

Let me repeat—I take my day off. I take my vacation. I take my sabbatical every seven years. At the same time I work hard. I play hard. I work hard.

A church is a family. A family without fun does not stay together very long. When I get assigned to a church that is a little cranky or maybe having a little conflict, the two surest ways of getting a new direction are to do some mission work together and to go have some fun together. If you are not having some fun, you are most likely not overly effective. I decided a long time ago that if I was going to be a pastor, I was going to be real and I was going to have a little fun along the way. Are you having any fun as a pastor? If not, change something.

Interlude

Supercharge
Effectiveness

here are times we find churches that just seem to have it going on. They have a good pastor, good leaders, an engaged congregation, good worship, and good community connection and are growing in faithfulness and effectiveness. So what is it that makes these congregations so effective? What is going on behind the scenes to make all of this happen? What traits exist? At the intersection of the nine things an effective pastor does differently and the two traits of an effective congregation, there is a super-charge effect that kicks into gear. When these nine practices come together with the two traits, great things happen! It is the proverbial sweet spot of a church.

Have you ever experienced a situation in which a very effective pastor is partnered with a congregation that is not motivated, inwardly focused, and/or just plain cranky? Have you ever experienced a situation in which a very effective congregation is partnered with an ineffective pastor? Both of these scenarios are frustrating to the other party to say the least! Congregations with less than fully effective pastors can sometimes lose motivation or, worse yet, have people leave the congregation to attend elsewhere where they can engage and be effective or become un-churched. Pastors with less than effective congregations can feel like they're beating their heads against the wall. The interesting part of this equation is that when an ineffective congregation or an ineffective pastor is partnered with an effective one, there can be long-term ramifications for both. A congregation with an ineffective pastor sometimes take years or maybe even decades to rebuild leadership, community connection, and trust within their congregation. Pastors serving congregations that do not have the traits of effective churches sometimes lose their drive and motivation. In fact, sometimes pastors leave the ministry after such an experience of frustration. This is why it is so imperative for both pastors and congregations to be striving toward effectiveness continuously! Ineffective pastors or congregations can "infect" the other for years and sometimes decades to come!

In the next two chapters, we will describe the top two traits of effective congregations. Effective congregations "**get it**" and are "**permission-giving partners**." When these two congregational traits come together with a pastor engaged in the nine things effective pastors do differently as described in the previous nine chapters, WATCH OUT! Nine to the power of two multiplies into the effectiveness of eighty-one traits. Now folks, that is the power of multiplication! When multiplication of effective traits occurs with the synergy of the pastor AND congregation, multiplication for the kingdom occurs. And that is what we call effective and faithful ministry.

9

Two Traits of Effective Congregations

Chapter Ten

They Get It

Jesus came near and spoke to them, "I've received all authority in heaven and on earth. Therefore, go and make disciples of all nations, baptizing them in the name of the Father and of the Son and of the Holy Spirit, teaching them to obey everything that I've commanded you. Look, I myself will be with you every day until the end of this present age." (Matthew 28:18-20)

It is not about us. (Tex Sample)

Those verses in the Bible in the Gospel of Matthew sum up the life of the church as it was created to be and become. These verses very clearly instruct the church in its purpose and function—the very reason for its existence. Yet, so many congregations lose sight of their very purpose of existence. They sometimes become very inwardly focused and lose sight of reaching those in their mission field. They sometimes begin to believe the pastor is at their church to serve and care for them exclusively. They have become insular and have forgotten what Jesus told us: to go and make new disciples of Jesus Christ for the transformation of the world. They have forgotten or lost sight of the mission!

Congregations that "get it" are ones that have a heart for and focus on the mission. Without a doubt, everything they do is based on one of three things: (1) helping people in their congregation grow in their faith, (2) building relationships with the unchurched so that they might find a relationship with Jesus Christ, and (3) helping people change their communities and the world—to be a more just and compassionate society. Congregations that "get it" have an unquestionable passion and commitment to the mission.

Many congregations start with the "how." In other words, they know how they do what they do (such as worship, ministries, activities, events). Some congregations know "how" they differentiate themselves from other churches. Very few congregations know the "why" of what they do. Without knowing the "why," congregations get bogged down in the "whats" and the "hows," and often become frozen in time and unable to make needed changes. Congregations that "get it" understand the need to change the methods ("how") to stay on mission ("why"). Congregations that don't "get it" often have mission creep. In other words, they start changing the mission so they don't have to change the methods. Simon Sinek in his book *Start with Why* states, "We say WHAT we do, we sometimes say HOW we do it, but we rarely say WHY we do WHAT we do."[1]

Congregations that "get it" have a key group of leaders who are sold out for the mission of Jesus Christ. These leaders are mature disciples. They are spiritually grounded yet continue to grow in their faith. They serve with joy and gratitude. These leaders have a contagious spirit and therefore ignite the passion

---

1. Simon Sinek, *Start with Why: How Great Leaders Inspire Everyone to Take Action* (New York: Portfolio, 2011), 29.

of ministry within the rest of the congregation. They see their ministry as a privilege to carry out—not just "work" or what they are "supposed" to do. There is an unselfishness in their spirit to be about the work of the church and Jesus Christ.

Congregations that "get it" are able to tell their stories. Telling their stories consists of being able and comfortable in sharing where God is working in their lives. Their stories may be "lightning bolt" kind of stories, but more likely they are the recent everyday stories of God's blessings, lessons, and workings in their lives. This is why we wrote the book *Get Their Name*—to help equip people learning how to tell their stories. When Christians are comfortable in sharing their stories, others who are searching and new to their faith are in turn allowed to understand more quickly why people of faith choose a Christian life. These congregations are comfortable sharing their faith in service, small groups, worship, and the mission field.

Congregations that "get it" have the majority of their people living in the church's mission field. They have a heart for the people in the mission field. They immerse themselves in their community. They live there, shop there, eat there, and participate in recreational activities there. They don't drive into the church and mission field to visit on Sunday. The congregation must reflect the mission field. The congregation looks like, acts like, and lives like the mission field. These congregations know the demographics of their community because not only do they continuously study their mission field, they are entrenched in the mission field. They are deeply invested in the mission field and have a passion and commitment to it. We never know what size the congregation must become, but we do know it must reflect the mission field where the church building is located.

Congregations that "get it" have a strong connection to at least one nearby school. This connection is way beyond being anonymous donors of needed items such as school supplies, socks, weekend food, and so forth. This deep connection is personal. It's relational! Congregations serve lunches for the teachers. Congregations read to children. Congregations host theme parties for classrooms. Congregations pray for the administration and teachers by name (with permission). Congregations get involved in parent-teacher associations. Congregations tutor students. Congregations provide hospitality for the school play or back-to-school night. The list can go on and on. Congregations that "get it" create opportunities to be eyeball to eyeball with the people in the mission field to build authentic relationships with people over time.

Congregations that "get it" spend more time in the mission field than they spend in the church building. They realize that the people they are trying to reach will most likely not stroll into the church. They are out and about in the mission field investing in and building relationships with unchurched people. Congregations find innovative, fun ways to engage people in conversation and activities that allow relationships to develop naturally over time. They invest in activities that cost people in the mission field nothing and include no preaching, prayer, or pressure. They are simply offering themselves up in service or a fun activity to get to know people. Furthermore, these congregations do these things not only outside the church building, but most often off of church grounds. Congregations go into the mission field. They don't expect the mission field to come to them.

Congregations that "get it" have a process in place to gather names and invest in personal, relationship-building follow-up.

These names may come from outwardly focused events or casual conversations or through a variety of other methods. Following up requires commitment over a period of time. We must first invest in people before they know us and trust us. Authentic invitations don't come from strangers. Authenticity comes from being in relationship with those you know and trust. Congregations must have an intentional, personal process to collect names and follow up in order to build relationships over time with repeated encounters. Those encounters include being in prayer for that person daily, writing notes, making phone calls, sending e-mails, and so on. This includes checking in on people and asking if you can be helpful in any way. The messages and conversations are not about "selling" the church. Rather, the conversation is centered on investing in the new relationship and helping people find their next steps in the life of the congregation. The motivation is not getting butts in the pews and bucks in the plate. Rather the motivation and messages are about offering ourselves in relationship to others, showing genuine care and concern. It is about investing in others. Once a relationship is formed, then an authentic invitation can be extended. Those first invitations are best given to outwardly focused events and small groups, because these are easier, more comfortable entry points for the unchurched.

Congregations that "get it" realize every church has two mission fields. One mission field is the people who are a part of the congregation and already have a relationship with Jesus Christ. The second mission field consists of those who do not have a relationship with Jesus Christ. Congregations that "get it" serve both mission fields but concentrate their efforts on the mission field of the unchurched, realizing that when churched folks are working to reach the unchurched, they are not only fulfilling their mission, they are also experiencing faith development themselves.

Congregations that "get it" make themselves available for guests during the worship experience. They prepare for and expect guests each and every Sunday. Therefore, they participate joyfully and genuinely in the ministries that provide a top-rate experience for first-time guests and others new to the church. Participants may forego Sunday school class in order to be a greeter at the door for guests arriving early. They may forego conversations with close friends who are also part of the congregation in order to be hospitable to a guest before, during, and after worship. Congregations that "get it" see Sunday as being more about expecting, preparing, and receiving guests rather than being all about them. They might even hold their Sunday school class time on Tuesday evening at someone's home rather than at church before or after worship so that they can make themselves available for guests on Sunday.

In summary, **congregations that "get it" have a laser focus on the "why"!** They fully understand their mission as the Great Commission. They don't see this as a sacrifice, but rather their gift back to Jesus Christ for his love and saving grace. When you are around congregations that "get it," you will know it! There will be no question about it. When congregations "get it," there is such a spirit that fills the people and their church that it's simply undeniable and truly awesome to experience!

Chapter Eleven

They Are Permission-Giving Partners

The one who went down is the same one who climbed up above all the heavens so that he might fill everything.

He gave some apostles, some prophets, some evangelists, and some pastors and teachers. His purpose was to equip God's people for the work of serving and building up the body of Christ until we all reach the unity of faith and knowledge of God's Son. God's goal is for us to become mature adults—to be fully grown, measured by the standard of the fullness of Christ.

(Ephesians 4:10-13)

Effective congregations are permission-giving partners. So what does it mean for a pastor to partner with her or his congregation and a congregation to partner with their pastor? Let's first look at the Google definition of *partner*: "a person who takes part in an undertaking with another or others . . . with shared risks and profits. *synonyms*: colleague, associate, coworker, fellow worker, collaborator, comrade, teammate."[1]

---

1. "partner," Google, https://www.google.com/search?q=partner%3A&oq=partner%3A &aqs=chrome..69i57j69i58.398j0j4&sourceid=chrome&es_sm=91&ie=UTF-8.

Being partners in ministry means a pastor and congregation are working together in a common direction taking both the risks and rewards together along the way. Each partner knows their function and responsibility both collectively and individually. Each partner has the other one's back. A partnership is a relationship of cohesion working for a common goal, in a unified direction, and for the same intended outcome. When I (Kay) work with churches planning a particular activity, it always amazes me when I ask them about their intended outcome and get the deer-in-the-headlights look. No intended outcome or purpose has been stated or ever discussed. Other times, congregations experience mission drift. Mission drift can be described as a ministry or activity that, at one time, was missionally aligned but has lost the missional connection over time or is no longer culturally relevant. Many times congregations are not only missing purposes for their ministries, activities, and events but are also missing a clearly understood mission and vision. A congregation that does not fully understand their mission of making disciples and the unique way they go about doing it while living in the future (vision) is floundering. They are many times busy congregations, but they are doing things for the sake of action, tradition, and calendar rather than for a clearly understood purpose with an intended outcome. Yet, on the other hand, when the pastor and a congregation partner in the mission and vision, effective and faithful ministry occurs.

In partnerships, each partner is considered an equal player with equal buy-in, responsibility, authority, and voice. This means that a congregation must also take responsibility for the outcomes of the church's ministries. Nothing is the sole responsibility of the pastor. Nothing is the sole responsibility of the congregation. No one partner has the louder voice. No one partner has a higher buy-in than the other. There is equal footing for both the risks and the rewards.

When effective ministry is taking place, leaders and pastors are working on the same team. The leaders have the back of the pastor. At the same time, the leaders hold the pastor accountable for leading the congregation in step with its stated mission and vision. Effective ministry occurs when the leaders and pastors are in synchronized steps with one another working in the same direction. The leaders and pastor are all communicating the same message with the same language to the rest of the congregation. There is one unified voice in a way forward. Now this is not to say that there are not lively conversations when the leadership team comes together! Quite the contrary! Fierce, spirited, and passionate conversations are always a part of an effective church. But the spirit of the conversation is one of collaboration in moving together in the mission and vision. It is not an adversarial or confrontational spirit. It is a conversation where ALL feel the responsibility to Jesus Christ for the church being faithful and effective and are therefore trying to puzzle through the best way to accomplish this. But no matter what the conversation is within the leadership team, the team and pastor come away from it with one unified voice and direction.

Effective congregations are not necessarily congregations that are conflict-free. If there is not some form or degree of conflict, the congregation and leaders are probably not pushing the envelope as much as they could for even more effective ministry. Congregations are many times conflict resistant. In other words, they are prone to value their personal relationships with others in the congregation more than being faithful to Jesus Christ for the mission. Pushing the envelope (being creative, innovative, risk-taking) creates tension, but many times it is in the tension that the most effective ministry happens. Leaders just have to make sure there is enough tension to move the church ahead without creating too much tension, which could be destructive to the congregation and thus the mission. Congregations must not avoid conflict. Effective congregations know how to manage conflict in a healthy manner. They embrace conflict as opportunities for growth and change.

Effective congregations are permission-giving congregations. That is, they give permission to their pastors and staff to carry out their ministry within healthy boundaries. Effective congregations not only have clearly understood and communicated mission and vision, but they also have congregational goals. The goals are assigned to the pastors and staff (paid and unpaid) to carry out in the day-to-day ministries (strategies). The leaders don't micromanage the pastor and staff. Rather the leaders ask for reports on the goal attainment from the pastor. The strategies of how the goals are accomplished are decided upon by the pastor and staff, not by the congregational leaders. Effective churches are permission-giving. They clearly outline the expectations (goals) of their pastor and staff, but leave it to the pastor and staff to execute them (the how/strategies).

Rev. Jeff Brinkman at Woods Chapel UMC in Lee's Summit, Missouri, has built a great culture of permission-giving for his lay ministry.

> The culture is all about missional alignment coupled with the freedom to "go and do" without lots of constraints. It's a system of "yes" more than "no." It is a culture of trying things

rather than constricting things. As long as it is *on mission*, experimenting is seen as a good thing. Trying something new and changes to common practices are common and cultural. In a world where churches commonly say things like, "We have never done it like that before," at Woods Chapel, members are encouraged to hear God's call and live out their ministry dreams for the Kingdom.

In his book *Just Say Yes: Unleashing People for Ministry*, Bishop Robert Schnase lists the traits of a permission-giving leader (and congregation).

Permission-giving leaders . . .

- trust people

- trust that God is at work in people and processes

- are initiators

- are responsible risk takers

- grow their churches by multiplication and not just by addition

- understand the importance of big strategies and long-term planning and broad participation for large projects

- know how to listen

- work with a minimum of defensiveness and territoriality

- get out of the way

- hold high expectations

91

- are clear about the mission and confident about the future

- seldom say no when presented with a new idea

- set high-performing staff and volunteers free, entrust them with more responsibilities, and offer them more opportunities

- know that exercising too much control limits the creativity and capacity of staff and volunteers

- work with flexible job descriptions in their supervision of others seeing that the essentials are done well and giving space for people to follow their callings, explore ideas they are curious about, and experiment with new approaches

- never go it alone

- open options rather than close them

- have the ability to say yes even to people who think differently than they do about issues

- develop habits that keep them freshly engaged with young people, new people, visitors, and those who do not yet belong to the church

- value the initiatives of laity as well as pastors, staff, or committee members[2]

---

2. Robert Schnase, *Just Say Yes: Unleashing People for Ministry* (Nashville: Abingdon, 2015), 96–99.

Bishop Schnase describes the need for changing attitudes and behaviors that can take away the constraints and move us into being a permission-giving church:

> Congregations and operational systems never become more permission-giving than the people who lead them. Leaders have a disproportionate influence on the culture and content of a church, and on the processes that either restrain or multiply ministries. They can discourage innovation, resist change, tighten rules, and ignore the gifts and callings of people. Or they can cultivate innovation and creativity and encourage people to discern and follow their callings to serve. Leaders foster openness to initiatives, or they squeeze people into the models of ministry they prefer. A willingness to let God change us and a desire to adapt our attitudes serve as prerequisites to lasting change. Permission-giving churches cannot thrive without permission-giving leaders.[3]

Permission-giving is sometimes scary for congregations. They may have had some bad experiences and have therefore created greatly tightened procedures. Sometimes they are tightened down so much that ministry just can't happen or it can't happen in a timely, effective manner. Effective congregations are permission-giving, but they certainly have proper processes and systems in place to promote this permission-giving ministry. In other words, there are policies and procedures in place that provide healthy boundaries for everyone to work within. This allows for trust to build for both the pastor and the congregation along with the staff and leaders. Trust can flourish when there is a system of checks and balances creating a protective playing field

3. Ibid., 93.

with boundaries. For example, the leaders and pastor of a congregation may set a goal for there to be X% increase in children and youth participation in the coming school year. The pastor will work with the staff (paid and unpaid) responsible for those areas of ministry. This may include a children's ministry coordinator and a youth coordinator. The pastor will clearly outline the percentage of increase that is expected in each area of ministry in order to accomplish the overall church goal. In turn, those two ministry team leaders are given the budget, responsibility, and authority to carry out the ministry they believe will create the growth desired. The pastor holds the staff accountable for the strategies created by the staff to meet the church goal while in turn the leadership team holds the pastor accountable for the goal only. Effective congregations have leadership teams that are permission-giving. They don't mire themselves in the details (strategies). They keep in focus a broader view of the church, which is mission, vision, and goals.

Effective congregations that are permission-giving partners with their pastors create a healthy organization that is not only vital to those inside the organization but also vital to those in the community, the mission field. Permission-giving partnerships allow for pastors, leaders, staff, and congregations to be nimble, flexible, energized, and effective.

Conclusion

It is important to know your "why." Why bother trying new things? Why bother trying to improve your skill set? Why try to revive a dying church? Why try to impact a secular and broken world? Why is it worth the risk? Do you know your "why"? I think the great genius (the "why") of the Wesleyan movement within Christianity was John and Charles Wesley's foundational passion to combine together the Great Commandment, the Great Compassion, and the Great Commission. When you combine these three foundational scriptures you get what I refer to as the real heart of the Wesley movement. We believe it was a part of the Wesley's "why" and it has certainly become a part of our "why," and we believe it has relevance for the broader church even beyond the Wesleyan movement.

The first of these three scriptures is often known as the Great Commandment:

> Jesus replied, "The most important one is *Israel, listen! Our God is the one Lord, and you must love the Lord your God with all your heart, with all your being, with all your mind, and with all your strength.*" (Mark 12:29-30)

I think this is where John Wesley picked up his passion for worship and preaching and his overall spirit of enthusiasm. So much so, that in the beginning of the Methodist movement, we were called enthusiasts. I think this is where it all begins . . . in the *heart*, as it began for John Wesley. He had all the educational training he could want at Oxford University, but it was the Aldersgate Street experience that changed the trajectory of John Wesley's life. It was a heartfelt experience for John Wesley, as he expressed in his journal for May 24, 1738: "I felt my heart strangely warmed."[1] Moving in, showing up, and a bias for action were early Wesleyan traits that Wesley derived from the Great Commandment. But he did not stop there; he combined his enthusiasm with an intellectual, thinking approach to faith: love the Lord God with your mind as well as with your heart and soul. Wesley insisted that his new pastors read, learn, and fine-tune their trade. He used an apprentice model of learning. The great genius is that he combined the head (thinking Christianity) with the soul (enthusiasm)! Once again, we need to do the same.

Second, it is very clear that John Wesley was committed to the second half of the Great Commandment, which I like to call the Great Compassion:

"The second is this, *You will love your neighbor as yourself.* No other commandment is greater than these."

The legal expert said to him, "Well said, Teacher. You have truthfully said that God is one and there is no other besides him. And to love God with all of the heart, a full understanding, and all of one's strength, and to love one's neighbor as oneself is much more important than all kinds of entirely burned offerings and sacrifices." (Mark 12:31-33)

---

1. John Wesley quoted in Steven W. Manskar, "Aldersgate," *Wesleyan Leadership*, May 24, 2011, http://wesleyanleadership.com/2011/05/24/aldersgate/.

At every turn, John Wesley, and later the early Methodist movement in America, demonstrated a deep compassion for those in need. They started schools, schools, and more schools due to believing that education was a way to help redeem and lift people out of poverty. John and the early Methodists started orphanages, hospitals, food banks, and a whole host of other ministries to help lift people out of poverty. This is another layer to his genius, combining the social gospel and the gospel of redemption. Some people believe Wesley helped England avert a revolution because of his work and success with helping lift up the poor. In America, I believe the early Methodists helped create the middle class by lifting the poor up to be the working class. Frances Asbury and the early Methodists convinced average people that their lot in life could change and they could become leaders in the new democracy. Traits associated with the work ethic, connecting together, and reaching outside the church to those in need are all derived from the Great Compassion. In fact, I don't think you can ever get to the Great Commission without first demonstrating a Great Compassion in your community.

This brings us finally to the Great Commission:

> Therefore, go and make disciples of all nations, baptizing them in the name of the Father and of the Son and of the Holy Spirit, teaching them to obey everything that I've commanded you. Look, I myself will be with you every day until the end of this present age. (Matthew 28:19-20)

The Great Commission drove John Wesley into open-field preaching, the coal mines, the sweatshops, and the streets and byways of England. It is also clear that as Wesley sent missionaries to America, it was out of a conviction that Christians must spread the gospel to new people—the Great Commission. The outwardly focused traits of effective pastors identified in this book and the ability of a congregation to understand its mission ("they get it") and be permission-giving enough to go outside its walls to reach a people they do not know for a result they might not see are absolutely based in a commitment to the Great Commission.

We believe the ingredients contained within the nine things effective pastors do differently and the two traits of effective congregations identified here are interwoven in an understanding of and conviction in the Great Commandment, the Great Compassion, and the Great Commission. When we see a church and a pastor in their sweet spot being effective (or however else you want to describe it), we believe it is due to the combination of these traits standing on the foundation of the Great Commandment, Compassion, and Commission. These together create the "X-factor"!

Are you born a leader or is it an acquired set of skills? Our answer is an absolute YES. It is both. Personality certainly plays a role in one's ability to lead. This is why in the Missouri Annual Conference we ask people to complete and study a variety of personality and leadership profiles like DiSC, StrengthsFinder, Meyers Briggs, and some of the new understandings of emotional quotient. Understanding who you are (being self-aware and self-reflective) and whose you are (being self-differentiated and grounded) are both extremely important. All this plays a role in the leader you are, but learned behaviors and skills define the leader you can become. If you look at Wesley's life, you will find he was groomed to be a leader primarily by Susanna Wesley, his mother. In addition, he was certainly schooled and groomed to be a leader at Oxford University. But it was his set of practices, ways of life, teachings, and behaviors that created a movement around the world that is still alive more than two hundred years later and has affected millions of lives.

Pastors, leaders, and congregations often find themselves doing the same thing over and over and over again hoping that by just trying a bit harder they may have a better or more significant outcome. Yet, the whole trajectory of a pastor's or congregation's ministry can dramatically change by adopting and practicing some new traits to be more effective. If a pastor and/or congregation would continuously work on taking steps to adopt the traits outlined in this book, year after year, watch out! Great things could happen! It is our hope that by doing these nine things differently, pastors will become more effective and have more impact in their ministries. It is also our hope that congregations will open themselves up in developing the two essential traits that not only help a congregation flourish but provide a setting for pastors to be as effective as possible. We have seen and experienced that when these two things come together, amazing, effective ministry can occur. We pray that the pastors reading this book will create two or three new habits that when practiced over time will create a more effective ministry. We pray that the congregations reading this book will adopt and practice the two traits of effective congregations to reach more people for Jesus Christ—for that's what is at the core of this book and our work: effectiveness for both pastors and congregations in living out the mission of making disciples of Jesus Christ for the transformation of the world.

> One of them, a legal expert, tested him. "Teacher, what is the greatest commandment in the Law?"

He replied, "You must love the Lord your God with all your heart, with all your being, and with all your mind. This is the first and greatest commandment. And the second is like it: You must love your neighbor as you love yourself. All the Law and the Prophets depend on these two commands." (Matthew 22:35-40)

We circle back once again to our introductory question. The question still remains, are you a born leader or is it an acquired skill set that one can learn? We have repeatedly and confidently said the answer is YES. It is both. Some things come to us naturally and other things are learned. Some things are easily learned, other things are very difficult to learn and may take a considerable amount of time to learn. If the traits described in this book did not come to you naturally, then they are traits that must be learned, adapted, and applied. In order to move into practicing these effective traits for pastors and congregations, it might be helpful to understand learning through the Four Stages of Competency or the conscious competence learning model.

Here is how Wikipedia describes these stages:

In psychology, the **four stages of competence**, or the "conscious competence" learning model, relates to the psychological states involved in the process of progressing from incompetence to competence in a skill. . . . The Four Stages of Learning provides a model for learning. It suggests that individuals are initially unaware of how little they know, or unconscious of their incompetence. As they recognize their incompetence, they consciously acquire a skill, then consciously use it. Eventually, the skill can be utilized without it being consciously thought through: the individual is said to have then acquired unconscious competence.[2]

We are sure you are asking what learning models have to do with this book. Here is the connection. It is important to understand how you learn. People learn using many different methods and styles. You need to find the best style or method for you. You need to be self-aware to know not only how you learn but also what you need to learn. What are your strengths? Where are your gaps? A coach may help you identify these things.

After working with pastors across the country, we know these are the basic nine traits effective pastors do differently. After working with hundreds of churches across the country, we have identified the two traits congregations need to practice to be effective. Now you know those traits. What is next? Knowing the traits is only the beginning. We must be intentional about developing the traits and practicing the traits. So what's next in your effectiveness development? Step one is to identify the traits that come naturally. Second, identify what you need to work on. Which ones need some work? Which ones need lots of work? Take some time to assess. Realize that most of these traits are skills acquired over a course of time. Remember, in our introduction we quoted Dr. Henry Cloud's book *Nine Things a Leader Must Do*. He writes about these realizations he had about leaders:

People who found what they were looking for in life seemed to do a certain set of things in common.

---

2. "Four Stages of Competence," Wikipedia, https://en.wikipedia.org/wiki/Four _stages_of_competence (accessed August 28, 2015).

If you were not born with these patterns for leadership in place, you can learn them.[3]

So then, pastors, do some self-reflection. Gather some people who know you well and can openly speak the truth so that you can begin to follow some new practices. So then, congregational leaders, gather a team and look at the two traits of an effective congregation and honestly evaluate how well your congregation tends to the traits of effective congregations. Which of these traits are second nature? Which traits were not on your radar at all? Which traits do you know you are practicing or not practicing well (conscious learning)? Which traits are you working on and moving into the consciously skilled area? In what areas do you need some training? In what areas do you need some coaching? What areas might you need both training and coaching? There is always room for improvement for us individually and as a congregation. What area will you work on first? How will you address becoming more effective and competent? What tools do you need? Who inside the church can help? Who from outside the church can help?

Remember, congregations, if a pastor comes to your church practicing the nine traits and your congregation is not practicing the two traits of "getting it" and "permission-giving," it would be like Jesus's parable of seeds falling on hard ground rather than fertile soil. We have many times seen effective pastors going into churches that didn't practice these two traits and meeting with resistance and conflict rather than being able to use their effectiveness for the kingdom. In other words, the pastor did not find

3. Henry Cloud, *Nine Things a Leader Must Do* (Nashville: Integrity House, 2006), 10.

fertile ground to sow the seeds of effectiveness. How fertile is the ground in your church to receive an effective pastor?

> He said many things to them in parables: "A farmer went out to scatter seed. As he was scattering seed, some fell on the path, and birds came and ate it. Other seed fell on rocky ground where the soil was shallow. They sprouted immediately because the soil wasn't deep. But when the sun came up, it scorched the plants, and they dried up because they had no roots. Other seed fell among thorny plants. The thorny plants grew and choked them. Other seed fell on good soil and bore fruit, in one case a yield of one hundred to one, in another case a yield of sixty to one, and in another case a yield of thirty to one. Everyone who has ears should pay attention." (Matthew 13:3-9)

And remember, pastors, if you have arrived at a congregation that is fertile (practicing the two traits), you are apt to find a congregation that has expectations for a strong, effective leader from the very start. If you have not equipped yourself to be an effective leader, you may very well encounter a frustrated congregation. In fact, the fertile soil may even begin to dry and harden. If there is fertile soil, but you don't sow seeds of effectiveness, you will indeed reap what you sow—ineffective ministry. How well do you sow the seeds of effectiveness by practicing the nine traits?

> Those who are taught the word should share all good things with their teacher. Make no mistake, God is not mocked. A person will harvest what they plant. Those who plant only for their own benefit will harvest devastation from their selfishness, but those who plant for the benefit of the Spirit will

harvest eternal life from the Spirit. Let's not get tired of doing good, because in time we'll have a harvest if we don't give up. So then, let's work for the good of all whenever we have an opportunity, and especially for those in the household of faith. (Galatians 6:6-10)

When an effective (practicing the nine things) pastor serves an effective (practicing the two traits) congregation, we get fruit from the mission field.

So we repeat, it is important to know your "why." For our part, we reconnected with the "why" of the Wesleyan movement. There was no doubt that Wesley knew his "why." Pastor, what is your "why"? Knowing your "why" helps connect you to your purpose. Knowing your purpose leads to your passion. Passion then drives your desire to be the most effective pastor possible. It is in effectiveness that you live out your full potential, becoming all that God has created you to be and do. Why do you do what you do? Pastor, it is important to know the things you need to practice over and over in your ministry to be effective.

Congregations, what is your "why"? What drives you? We believe the "why" for congregations has already been given to us. We don't need to figure it out. We don't need to spend months meeting about it. Jesus told us in the Gospel of Matthew that the purpose of a church is to make disciples. What churches must spend time on is figuring out the unique way they accomplish the mission—this is their vision. Then they need to set annual goals in order to live into the vision to accomplish the mission. Congregations, how well understood are your mission and vision? What work needs to be completed in order for them to be widely understood and be a guide for everything the church does?[4]

It is important to know as a congregation the need to be open to the leadership of an effective pastor. We must be open to new ideas. We must be open to connecting with our mission field. We must know our context and be relevant to the people in our context. We have to be culturally relevant! Being culturally relevant is a moving target. It is something we must consistently evaluate, making necessary changes with any cultural shifts. An effective pastor will be able to help a congregation navigate through shifts if the congregation is open to an effective pastor.

It is our hope that this book proves to be a helpful resource in identifying, defining, and evaluating these nine things effective pastors do differently and the two traits effective congregations do differently. Pastors, we hope this will be a helpful resource for your continued development as a pastor. We also hope it helps you understand the two traits of an effective congregation and aids you in resourcing and supporting your congregation in its development. Congregations, we hope this will be a helpful resource in being an effective, competent, and compelling church. We also hope it helps you understand the nine traits of effective pastors and assists you in resourcing and supporting your pastor in his or her development.

We believe that by working together, pastors and congregations can continuously learn, develop, and strive towards effectiveness to reach more people for Jesus Christ. Our prayer is that through working together, every pairing of pastor and

---

4. See more about mission, vision, and strategic ministry planning in our book *10 Prescriptions for a Healthy Church* (Nashville: Abingdon, 2015).

congregation can indeed create this "X-factor" of effectiveness and be all that God has created you to be, become, and do to reach the mission field for Jesus Christ.

Blessings in your journey,

Bob & Kay

Additional Resources to Help Your Congregation

9^2

It's All about Relationships

Excerpt from *Get Their Name*

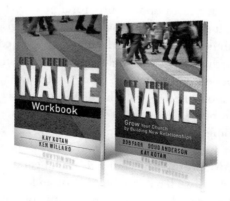

I n every church, every pastor and all leaders say they want their congregation to grow. Yet we struggle mightily with what appear to be some strong obstacles. In spite of our desire, we are experiencing the fact that about 80 percent of our congregations are either plateaued, slowly declining, or rapidly declining. Though there are many facets of the life of any given congregation one could improve, it is obvious we are not connecting with people we don't know outside our congregations. If we don't figure out how to connect with new people and the mission field around our buildings, the other facets of the life of the congregation are all for naught. We will continue to lose ground and decline. It is easy to get bogged down in the day-to-day operation of running our church. We lose sight of our purpose, our priorities, and the very mission of the church: build relationships with God, with one another, and with other people we don't know.

The first step in reaching new people we do not know is to create and extend radical hospitality beyond the church walls. Hospitality is a part of extending ourselves in relationships. Hospitality creates an opportunity for a new relationship to be built. Hospitality is crafted in an outwardly focused culture of the community of faith. Evangelism is often defined as an invitation to church. Stop it! We would define evangelism as an invitation to experience God through Jesus Christ. Evangelism is very much a one-on-one process. The first step of evangelism is not the church, but a relationship. The only way the nonbelieving world is going to give us (disciples) a chance is if we build trust through an authentic relationship. We are no longer living in a church-centric world. The church is no longer a valued institution. Therefore, we have to rebuild trust and value with people we do not know. That begins through one-on-one trusting relationships. Through a trusting relationship, you might have the opportunity to share your faith and bring someone back to the gathered community of faith in hopes that the Holy Spirit would move that person's life for a life-changing experience. It is still true that most people find their faith with the help of another person. We think the sequence of evangelism that we need to learn is the following: get the person's name (without being weird), have a conversation, and build an authentic relationship over time, leading to a moment when you can share your faith and to a chance to bring the person back to the gathered community of faith. We will let the Holy Spirit take it from there!

In our consulting work with churches through the Healthy Church Initiative process and other workshops across the country, we continually encounter some common myths about evangelism in the twenty-first century. We could probably name twenty, but here are the top five:

- Evangelism means inviting people to church.

- If people will just come into the building, they will see how nice we are and will want to return.

- If we do good deeds in our community, people will see it and want to come to our church.

- Everybody I know already goes to church.

- If we just had the right program, everyone would want to come to church.

Here are some best practices of effective evangelism to counter the myths above:

- Invitation flows from an authentic relationship. It is about experiential faith-sharing—not church-selling.

- If you are going to use the building for community activities, ask how you will follow up and build relationships with the people coming into your building.

- If you are going to do good deeds in the community, follow the good deeds to the house. In other words, get to know the people you are helping. Invest in them—the people—not just the service.

- It may be true that everybody you know already goes to church. Where are you willing to hang out to meet people who do not go to church? At least half of the population in every state in America does not have an active faith. Surely you can find a new person or two to build a relationship.

- People don't come to church because of a program. People come to church for a genuine experience that gives their life hope and grace.

We ran into a pivotal moment of truth for ourselves as transformational leaders. We consistently challenge churches to build relationships with the people in their own community so they might come to know Christ. On one particular occasion, an older congregant confronted us. He told us we had asked him to reach people in a new way. He had never been equipped to do so. Most importantly, he could not fathom a way to do this without feeling weird or being seen as weird by the other person. That very conversation set in motion our desire to help congregations once again become familiar with a faith-sharing process that is not so scary.

Over the past eight years, we have been working the Healthy Church Initiative transformation process throughout the country. In those hundreds of consultations, we discovered that churches have some very common blind spots. In fact, we compiled the recommendations to help congregations reach new people in the twenty-first century, published as *10 Prescriptions for a Healthy Church*.[1] Most of our recommendations cause us to rethink "doing church," imagining it in a way we might never have before. It causes us to get outside our walls and learn to be contextually relevant with our neighbors. It causes us to get outside our comfort zone of having "them" come to us and instead has us going to be a part of them.

We encourage you to sit down with other leaders in your church and evaluate how your church is doing when it comes to building relationships—with one another, with Christ, and with new folks. Where are the gaps? What do you need to start doing differently?

---

1. Bob Farr and Kay Kotan, *10 Prescriptions for a Healthy Church* (Nashville: Abingdon, 2015).